Sabine Baring-Gould

The Silver Store, Collected from Mediæval Christian and Jewish Mines

Sabine Baring-Gould

The Silver Store, Collected from Mediæval Christian and Jewish Mines

ISBN/EAN: 9783337032449

Printed in Europe, USA, Canada, Australia, Japan

Cover: Foto ©Lupo / pixelio.de

More available books at **www.hansebooks.com**

THE SILVER STORE

COLLECTED FROM

MEDIÆVAL CHRISTIAN AND

JEWISH MINES.

BY

S. BARING-GOULD, M.A.

AUTHOR OF 'CURIOUS MYTHS OF THE MIDDLE AGES,'
ETC.

LONDON:
LONGMANS, GREEN, AND CO.
1868.

DEDICATED

TO

THE RIGHT HONOURABLE

THE VISCOUNTESS DOWNE.

PREFACE.

IN a former work, 'Post-Mediæval Preachers,' the author drew attention to a class of ancient writers who are rarely studied, and whose very names are known only to the book-hunter. From these and kindred sources, and also from the Talmud, the majority of the legends and anecdotes in this volume have been drawn.

No apology is offered for introducing them to the public. It is not in the power of many to toil through ponderous tomes, written in languages with which they are not familiar; and it is proper for those who have facility and leisure for this study, to employ what they have acquired for the public good.

The author thinks it only fair to himself to add, that some of the most *piquant* stories in this collection are, in their original form, wholly devoid of point.

It has afforded the writer no little pleasure to bring, like Goldner, roses of gold out of the gloomy, tangled overgrowth of Mediæval fancy and superstition, in the hopes that the drudgery and routine of nineteenth century life may not have dulled the keenness of public perception of the beautiful and pure and true.

Some may object to the introduction of lighter pieces at the end of the book ; but the 'Silver Store' would not have fairly represented the genial, laughter-loving, as well as moral and devout temper of the ages which invented these tales, had the element of grotesqueness been excluded. The droll and the lovely were strangely intermixed and wonderfully blended in the Mediæval mind, as is instanced in the architectural masterpieces of the middle ages, where the quaint gurgoyle harmonizes with the angel and the flower.

Two or three of the humorous pieces at the end of the volume certainly hit the ladies rather hard. It must be remembered by forbearing and forgiving woman, that the perpetrators of these stories were confirmed old bachelors.

Lest the writer should be supposed to sympathise with these ungenerous attacks, he has appended in the notes the originals on which the verses are based, which will

Preface. ix

clear him of the imputation of having invented these libels, and will afford the curious choice specimens of monkish Latin.

Let the fair sex remember also, that, where the writer has been free to express his own sentiments, as in Dr. Bonomi, he has not spared the lords of creation, and that compensation is offered in the former part of the volume. Surely Beruriah* and Ruth will make amends for Mrs. Malone and the Judge's wife. A few of the pieces in the 'Silver Store' have already appeared in 'Fraser's Magazine,' and one in 'Temple Bar.'

* By an oversight, in 'The Loan,' the name Beruriah has been spelt incorrectly.

Dalton, Thirsk:
March 1, 1868.

CONTENTS.

	PAGE
THE DEVIL'S CONFESSION	1
THE BUILDING OF S. SOPHIA	9
HADAD	17
ROBIN REDBREAST'S CORN	22
THE RABBI JOACHIM	26
THE TWO SIGNS	31
TURN AGAIN	33
POPE BONIFACE VIII.	40
GOLDNER	44
THE LITTLE SCHOLAR	50
THORKELL-MANI	54
A PARABLE	57
BLIND AUSTIN	58

	PAGE
LANCELOT 65	
THE SWALLOWS OF CITEAUX . . . 69	
POOR ROBIN 74	
THE OLIVE TREE 78	
BISHOP BENNO AND THE FROGS . . . 81	
THE UNIVERSAL MOTHER 86	
THE LOAN 87	
DOCTOR FAUSTUS 93	
THE WIFE'S TREASURE . . . 99	
THE ARMS OF MAYENCE 102	
THE MASS FOR THE DEAD 107	
THE LUCK FLOWER 115	
THE THREE CROWNS 125	
THE RABBI'S SON-IN-LAW:	
I. THE WEDDING OF AKIBA 132	
II. THE MORROW OF THE WEDDING . . . 137	
III. THE RETURN 142	
THE MINER OF FALUN 148	

HUMOROUS POEMS.

	PAGE
THE DREAM OF THE HALTER .	153
THE TELESCOPE . . .	. 156
DOCTOR BONOMI	. 162
LIGHTENING THE VESSEL .	. 177
EX NIHILO NIHIL FIT . . .	. 180
THE SENTENCE ON THE THIEF .	187
NOTES	. 193

THE SILVER STORE.

THE DEVIL'S CONFESSION.

[CÆSARIUS HEISTERBACHENSIS,
De Miraculis et Visionibus sui Temporis, lib. iii. c. 26. A.D. 1230.]

THROUGH the tall minster windows of Cologne
The flaming saffron of the evening shone;
A golden dove, suspended in the choir,
It turned into a bird of living fire,
    Floating above the sacramental shrine.
It was the evening of that Maundy night,
When, in the ghastly glimmering moonlight,
The Saviour prostrate fell in sweat of blood,
And by His side an awe-struck angel stood,
    Wiping the pain-drops from the face divine.
In the confessionals, from hour to hour,
Sat the priests, wielding the absolving power,

And penitents were thronging all the fane,
Seeking release from the long gnawing pain
   Of conscience poisoned by the tooth of sin.
And many a sob broke out upon the still
Dim air, and sent an answering thrill
Through unlocked hearts; and, praying on their knees,
They bent, and waited their turn of release
   From horrors haunting the waste soul within.

A little space apart, with restless eyes,
Upon his face a blank look of surprise,
And on his brow a shadow of great dread—
Not kneeling, not erect, with out-thrust head—
   Stood a mute stranger in a nook of gloom,
Where lay a prelate with a seven-clasped book,
And, in one hand, a floreate pastoral crook,
   Sculptured in alabaster on his tomb.
The stranger's dress was carved with antique slash,
Around his waist was knotted a red sash,
   And in his bonnet danced a scarlet plume.
He was a fallen spirit. Now he saw,
In a wild flutter of hope, hate, and awe,
Souls that were blackened with guilt's deepest stain
Pass to their shriving, and come forth again

Assoiled and white ; then caught a distant ring
Of angels chanting, 'To the Lamb be praise
Who from the Book of Death doth sins erase
With His own blood ! O ecstacy untold !
When brought the lost sheep back into the fold,
 And found the coin marked with the image of the King

He thought, ' If these from chains are sent forth free,
Can there, O can there be a chance for me ?
That I, who long from Heaven have outcast been,
I who the joys of Paradise have seen,
 Flowing from union with a holy God ;
That I, who tasted have the woes of Hell,
Since before Michael's flashing lance I fell,
 And all the passages of gloom have trod,
Where burns the fire of an undying Hate,
Burning to strangle, scorch, and suffocate,
And Envy's worm feeds ever; where,
Horror of all, is unrelieved Despair ;
That I, like these, may also go forth shriven,
Once more become a denizen of Heaven !'

When the last foot was gone, and all the aisle
Was silent, he stepped forth with leer of guile,

And, gliding down to a confessional, brushed
In by a priest in meditation hushed,
  And said :
            ' To thee will I unclose my sin
Of lawless thought, and word, and evil deed,
That I, of all the consequences freed,
  When the bright doors are open, may pass in.'
Then said the priest, ' Begin, in God's trine Name.'
' I have a hitch of speech, and cannot frame
  The words in German.'
                'Then in thine own tongue.'
The Devil muttered, with a sort of scoff :
' Nomine Dagon, Beelzebub, Ashtaroth.
My sins, O father ! are of deepest dye,
They bar me out from tranquil courts on high,
  Where endless anthems to my God are sung.'
Then from his lips was his confession hissed ;
It was of crimes a long appalling list.
But he only had advanced a little way
Ere the confessor ordered, angry : ' Stay !
Thou art not kneeling, son, that I can see.'
' Father, there's something crooked in my knee.'
' Go on then,' said the priest, in lower tone.
' I've sinned exceedingly, through fault my own,

Have wakened up in peaceful families strife,
Have urged the husband on to hate the wife,
  And the child bade against its parents rise.
The thief I prompted to his villany ;
The adult'rous flame was kindled hot by me ;
  I turned the glances of malignant eyes ;
As sower, sowed in families mistrust ;
And Friendship cankered I with Envy's rust ;
The murderer I prompted to his deed
I roused the insatiable money greed—
Mens' eyes I dazzled with the blink of gold,
And taught that Heaven could be bought and sold ;
  And faith I staggered, planting weeds of doubt.
The sland'rous lie by me was deftly wrought ;
Pure minds I sullied with polluting thought,
  Working like leaven.'
                  Here fiercely he laughed out.
A hideous burst of wild discordant laughter
Shaking the wall, and quivering in each rafter,
  And flung in echoes all along the roof.
The old confessor starting, terrified,
Said : 'In the sacred Name of Him who died,
Profane one ! outrage not the holy rite !'
' Pardon me, father, pray ; my breast I smite.

I have convulsions, but at thy reproof
The fit is passed.   And now let me proceed.'
Then he unfolded many a godless deed,
And muttered on an hour, and was not done,
So the confessor stopped him, saying. 'Son,
Thou couldst not crowd these many actions in
A hundred years of unremitted sin.'
' A hundred times ten hundred, rather say,
Labouring at crime, unflagging, night and day,
　　Through all the ages from the hour I fell.'
Shuddered the priest and made the holy sign :
· In the Name of God, and of His Son divine,
　　Who art thou ? answer.'
　　　　　　　　　　　　' A spirit lost of hell.'
The priest leaped up with an affrighted cry :
· Angels of Jesus, stand me succouring by.'
Then he relapsed, and laid aside his dread :
' Why hast thou sought this sacrament ? ' he said ;
　　' Wherefore these horrors to my ear reveal ? '
' I saw thee vested with a wondrous might,
To make the sons of darkness heirs of light,
Blackest of souls become as drifted snow ;
And, to the sentence of the priest below
　　The Judge of all things setteth to His seal.

Then thought I : Oh ! if shattered were my chain,
I might the gates of Paradise regain.
   Say, is there any gleam of hope for me ? '

' I know the mercy of the Crucified
Is very lofty, deep, exceeding wide ;
Then if thy sorrow only be sincere,
In the Lord's name, I bid thee have no fear ;
   The blood of Christ will reach as far as thee.'

' Father, why question thou my strong desire
To fly the abysses of eternal fire,
And from keen misery obtain release,
And refuge in the home of endless peace ?
There comes a thrill on me, as now I grope,
With feeble glimmer for a thread of hope.'

' Son, ere I utter the absolving word,
Of thy contrition I must be assured ;
Therefore on thee a penance I impose.'
' Give me ten thousand of acutest woes,
   And from my purpose, mark you, if I swerve,
Bid me be bound upon a flaming wheel,
Set with the sharpest blades of tempered steel,

Bid it revolve in fire at whirlwind speed,
Parch me, and lacerate, and make me bleed
 And suffer with the finest mortal nerve.
Turn into flaming drops my coursing tears,
Bid me thus writhe through fifty thousand years,
And I will hug the woe and not repine.'
'Son,' said the pastor, ' no such test be thine.
As thou didst fall through thy unbounded pride,
Bow to the figure of the Crucified
 But once, and utter with a broken sigh,—
" I am not worthy to look up to heaven ;
Oh, be free pardon to the rebel given." '
 ' What ? ' said the Devil, with an angry cry,
' Bow to a God so lost to sense of shame,
As to take human nature and man's name !
Bow to a God who could Himself demean
To suck the breast, and sweep the kitchen clean,
And saw up chips for Joseph ? One who died
Upon a gallows with a mangled side !
 Ha ! when another twist of Fortune's wheel
Would have sent me up, and cast Him below !
Ha! To the Son of Mary shall I bow?'
 And with a curse, he turned upon his heel.

THE BUILDING OF S. SOPHIA.

JUSTINIAN, Emperor and Augustus, bent
On the imperial city's due embellishment,
Whilst musing, sudden started up, and cried:
' There is no worthy minster edified
Unto the Ruler of earth, sea and skies,
The One eternal, and the only wise.
Solomon the Great a temple built of old
To the Omnipotent, at cost untold.
Great was his power, but mine must his surpass
As ruddy gold excels the yellow brass.
I too a costly church will dedicate,
To preach God's Majesty and tell my state.'

Then called the Emperor an artist skilled,
With sense of beauty and proportions filled,
And said, ' In the name of Wisdom, build.

Build of the best, best ways, and make no spare,
The cost entire my privy purse shall bear.
Solomon took gifts of gold, and wood, and stone,
But I, Justinian, build the church alone.
Then go, ye heralds! forth to square and street,
With trumpet blare, and everywhere repeat,
That a great minster shall erected be
By our august, pacific Majesty;
And bid none reckon in the work to share,
For we ourselves the whole expense will bear.'
And as Justinian lay that night awake,
Weary, and waiting for white day to break,
The thought rose up, 'Now when this flesh is dead,
My soul, by its attendant spirit led,
Shall hear the angel at the great gate call,
What ho! Justinian comes, magnifical,
Who to the Eternal Wisdom, uncreate,
A church did build, endow and consecrate,
The like of which by man was never trod:
Then rise, Justinian! to the realm of God.'

Now day and night the workmen build; apace
The church arises, full of form and grace;

The Building of S. Sophia.

The walls upstart, the porch and portals wide
Are traced, the marble benches down each side,
The sweeping apse, the basement of the piers;
The white hewn stone is laid in level tiers.
Upshoot the columns, then the arches turn,
The roof with gilded scales begins to burn.
Next, white as mountain snow, the mighty dome
Hangs like a moon above the second Rome.
Within, mosaic seraphs spread their wings,
And cherubs circle round the King of Kings,
On whirling wheels, besprent with myriad eyes;
And golden, with gold hair, against blue skies,
Their names beside them, twelve Apostles stand,
Six on the left, and six on the right hand.
And from a nimbus set with jewelled rays,
Looks calm, majestic down, the Saviour's face.
Fixed is the silver altar, raised the screen,
A golden network prinked red, blue, and green,
With icons studded, hung with lamps of fire;
And ruby curtained round the sacred choir.
Then, on a slab above the western door,
Through which, next day, the multitude shall pour,
That all may see and read, the sculptors grave:—
'This House to God, Justinian Emperor gave.'

And now, with trumpet blast and booming gong,
Betwixt long lines of an expectant throng,
The imperial procession sweeps along.
The saffron flags and crimson banners flare
Against the sweet blue sky above the square.
In front, the church of Hagia Sophia glows,
A pile of jewels set in burnished snows.

Begemmed, and purple wreathed, the sacred sign
Labarum moves, the cross of Constantine.
Then back the people start on either side,
As ripples past a molten silver tide
Of Asian troops in polished mail; next pass
Byzantine guards, a wave of Corinth brass.
And then, with thunder tramp, the Varanger bands
Of champions gathered from grey northern lands,
Above whom Odin's raven flaps its wing;
And, in their midst, in a gold-harnessed ring
Of chosen heroes, on a cream-white steed
In gilded trappings, of pure Arab breed,
To dedicate his church doth Cæsar ride
In all his splendour, majesty, and pride.
With fuming frankincense and flickering lights,
The vested choir come forth as he alights.

The Building of S. Sophia.

Now shrill the silver clarions loud and long,
And clash the cymbals, bellows hoarse the gong,
A wild barbaric crash. Then on the ear
Surges the solemn chanting, full and clear:
' Lift up your heads ye gates, and open swing
Ye everlasting doors before the King!'
Back start the valves—in sweeps the train,
Next throng the multitude the sacred fane.

Justinian entering, halts a little space,
With haughty exultation on his face,
And, at a glance, the stately church surveys.
Then reads above the portal of the nave —
' This House to God, Euphrasia widow gave.'
' What ho!' he thunders, with a burst of ire,
As to his face flashes a scarlet fire;
' Where is the sculptor? Silence, all you choir!
Where is the sculptor?'
                Ceases the choral song,
A hush falls instant on the mighty throng.
' Bring forth the sculptor, who yon sentence wrought;
His merry jest he'll find full dearly bought.'

Then fell before him, trembling, full of dread,
The graver. ' Cæsar, God preserved!' he said,

'I carved not that! exchanged has been the name
From that I chiselled.   I am not to blame.
This is a miracle, for no mortal hand
Could banish one and make another stand,
And on the marble leave nor scar nor trace,
Where was the name deep cut, it did efface.
Beside the letters, Sire! the stone is whole.'
'Ha!' scoffed the Emperor; 'now by my soul,
I deemed the sacred age of marvels passed away!'
Forth stepped the Patriarch and said, 'Sire, I pray,
Hearken!   I saw him carve, nor I alone,
Thy name and title which have fled the stone;
And I believe the finger was Divine
Which set another name and cancelled thine—
The finger that, which wrote upon the wall
Belshazzar's doom, in Babel's sculptured hall;
The finger that, which cut in years before,
On Sinai's top, on tables twain, the Law.'

Justinian's brow grew dark with wrath and fear:
'Who is Euphrasia widow, I would hear,
This lady who my orders sets at naught,
And robs me of the recompense I sought.
Who is Euphrasia?'

The Building of S. Sophia. 15

       But none spake a word.
' What! of this wealthy lady have none heard?'
Again upon the concourse silence fell,
For none could answer make, and tidings tell.
' What ! no man know ! Go some the city round,
And ask if such be in Byzantium found.'

Then said a priest, and faltered : ' Of that name
Is one, but old and very poor, and lame,
Who has a cottage close upon the quay;
But she, most surely, Sire, it cannot be.'

' Let her be brought.' Then some the widow seek,
And lead the aged woman, tottering, weak,
With tattered dress, and thin white straying hair,
Bending upon a stick, and with feet bare.

' Euphrasia,' said the monarch sternly, ' speak !
Wherefore didst thou my strict commandment break
Contributing, against my orders, to this pile ?'
The widow answered simply, with faint smile,
' Sire ! it was nothing, for I only threw
A little straw before the beasts which drew
The marble from the ships, before I knew

Thou wouldst be angry. Sire ! I had been ill
Three weary months, and on my window-sill
A little linnet perched, and sang each day
So sweet, it cheered me as in bed I lay,
And filled my heart with love to Him who sent
The linnet to me ; then, with full intent
To render thanks, when God did health restore,
I from my mattress pulled a little straw
And cast it to the oxen—I did nothing more.'

'Look !' said the Cæsar, 'read above that door !
Small though thy gift, it was the gift of love,
And is accepted of our King above ;
And mine rejected as the gift of pride
By Him who humble lived and humble died.
Widow, God grant hereafter, when we meet,
I may attain a footstool at thy feet!'

HADAD.

[1 Kings xi. 21.]

'WITH me what hast thou lackèd?' Pharaoh said,
As Hadad stood before him with bowed head
    And folded hands and downcast eyes.
'Here hast thou had in Egypt goodly lands,
Cornfields and pasture, and large servant bands,
    And all the heart of man should prize.
I have exalted thee next to the throne;
Of strangers thou art honoured, thou alone.
    Thou hast to wife the sister of my queen,
Tahpnes. Thy word must all attend;
Obsequious crowds must in thy presence bend;
    Thy vesture flashes with the jewels' sheen;
Thy chests are stored with gold; a goodly pile
Thy new white palace, mirrored in the Nile,
    With glittering courts and stately towers,

And colonnades above the sacred stream,
Which washes past them with a golden gleam,
    Watering thy gardens sweet with flowers.
What hast thou lacked, that thou wouldst fare away?'
'Nothing,' he answered; 'yet let me go, I pray.
Thou hast been good to me, ay, passing kind;
Yet, with enough to satisfy the mind,
    The heart is empty. Let me go!'
'What! hast thou not a dearly treasured wife,
Whose love is poured into thy cup of life,
    To fill thy heart to overflow,
Whose white arms lace thee to a faithful breast?
In a true woman's love is perfect rest.'
    'No, Sire!' said Hadad sadly, 'no!'
'What hast thou lackèd?' once more asked the King.
Then Hadad slowly raised his head. 'Nothing :
    Yet——let me go!
Sire! many years ago, a feeble child,
I was brought up in Edom's barren wild,
    Upon a hill-side, underneath a tent.
Before were soft brown hills, a gravelly dell,
Seven stately palm-trees by a leaking well;
    A torrent bed, the water spent.

I used to watch the morning sun arise
Over sharp mountain ridges, into skies
    Bluer than turquoise in this ring;
And floods of glory down the valleys rolled,
Turning the seven palms into palms of gold,
    And gilding birds on passing wing.
I heard the rock-doves calling with soft coo
Among the fragments where the wild pinks grew,
    And avens scrambled sunny-eyed.
I saw the jackal skulking to his lair,
And from the dewy herb upstart the hare,
    And lizards from their hollows glide;
And where white rocket to the cliffs would cling,
Danced sulphur butterflies on flickering wing.
    I watched the lively cricket leap,
And with the burnished beetle I would play,
Or climb the rocks for flowers—thus pass my day,
    Or steal into the shade to sleep.
Sire! I must Edom see again once more;
This land is exile, and my heart is sore,
    Thinking of Edom and the past.
As in my rustling silks my hall I pace,
I think not of its splendour, beauty, grace;
    Nothing my heart will satisfy.

I value not my riches, nor the pride
Of rank and rule; I but half love my bride.
 I must see Edom, or I die!
There lived my father and my mother'—his head,
As he spoke, sank lower—'but they are dead.
 O'er Edom Joab's fury rolled;
He swept our pleasant land with sword and flame,
Carried our sisters off to toil and shame,
 As slaves our little brothers sold.
The land was purpled with our people's blood,
Their carcasses were cast as vultures' food.
 I saw my aged father fall.
About him were my mother's sweet arms wound;
She lay with him upon the trampled ground.
 I spoke. She answered not my call!
There is a purple glen with shingle slides,
And mossy ledges where the gentian hides.
 There, in a narrow rock-hewn cell,
I laid them, gently sleeping, side by side,
Alone, with arms entangled, as they died.
 Years have gone by, and yet full well
I know the place where is their humble grave.
Above it, fragrant juniper bushes wave;
 Below it is a bubbling well.

At night I hear the raven's doleful cry,
And, starting, wake, and turn upon my bed and sigh,
    And think upon that lonely tomb.
I have no rest.   I made that grave alone,
Trembling and hastily—ill-secured the stone.
    And when the hyæna in the gloom
Snarleth, I fear——.'   Then his utterance failed.
And Pharaoh said, ' What thou hast now detailed
    Should be forgotten ; past recall
Are childish years.   Those things are lost for e'er
That made to thee thy barren Edom dear.
    There, thou hast nothing ; *here*, hast all.'
' Something there is.   Still is that mountain line,
The same birds and flowers ; and the same lights shine
    At morn and eve.   I know that slain,
Or gone, are those who clasped me in their arms ;
Hewn down by Joab are those seven green palms ;
    And yet, may be, their stumps remain.
And there are father's, mother's bones, I know.
Sire !—brother man !—I pray thee, let me go !'

ROBIN REDBREAST'S CORN.

In a quiet sheltered valley
　　Underneath a furzy hill,
Where their light from rocky ledges
　　Silver threads of water spill,

Patient Benedictine brothers
　　Thatch their cot with russet fern,
Singing 'Ave, Maris Stella!'
　　To the flowing of the burn.

They have come from southern regions
　　To the wastes of Finisterre,
Without scrip, or purse, or weapon,
　　Trusting in the might of prayer.

In a pleasant sunward hollow
    Of the barren purple fell,
They have built a rustic chapel,
    Hung a little tinkling bell.

There, alone in Christ believing,
    Wait the brothers God's good time,
When shall spread the Gospel tidings,
    Like a flood, from clime to clime.

Yonder is a Druid circle,
    Where the priests dance on the dew,
Singing of Ceridwen's kettle,
    And the ploughing of old Hu.

Now the brothers cut the heather,
    Stack the turf for winter fire,
Wall about with lichened moorstones
    The enclosure of their byre.

Next they drain a weedy marish,
    Praying in the midst of toil,
And with plough of rude construction
    Draw slight furrows through the soil.

Then seek wheat.—It was forgotten;
  All their labour seems in vain;
The barbarian Kelts about them
  Little knew of golden grain.

Said the Prior: 'God will help us
  In this hour of bitter loss.'
Then, one spied a Robin Redbreast
  Sitting on a wayside cross.

Doubtless came the bird in answer
  To the words the Prior did speak,
For a heavy wheat-ear dangled
  From the Robin's polished beak.

Then the brothers, as he dropped it,
  Picked it up and careful sowed,
And abundantly in autumn
  Reaped the harvest where they strewed.

Do you mark the waving glory
  O'er the Breton hill-slopes flung?
All that wealth from Robin Redbreast's
  Little ear of wheat has sprung.

Do you mark the many churches
  Scattered o'er that pleasant land?
All results are of the preaching
  Of that Benedictine band.

Therefore, Christian, small beginnings
  Pass not by with lip of scorn;
God may prosper them, as prospered
  Robin Redbreast's ear of corn.

THE RABBI JOACHIM. (1)

[*Talmud Berachot*, ix. fol. 60.]

THE RABBI JOACHIM, no little sore
At heart to see fair Bethlehem no more,
Went forth with staff in hand, and drooping head,
   And locked his door.

The Rabbi Joachim, whate'er befell,
Said: 'Man as God is not; he cannot tell
What is the best for him; but what God doth,
   He doeth well.'

He had grown old with Miriam, and none
Had seen them strive together. She was gone.
The Rabbi smote his breast: 'God doeth well
   What He hath done.'

The Rabbi Joachim.

There was to Joachim a little child :
It died. The Rabbi looked to heaven and smiled.
'What my God doth, He doeth well,' he said,—
    Reconciled.

Then there was famine, and the Rabbi fed
The starving poor with all his substance. Dead
Were all his kin. 'Why should I save?'
    The old man said.

And now he parted from his home, to fare,
Far off, with nothing his, save clothes to wear,
A faithful dog, a little lamp of oil,
    A book of prayer.

He journeyed till the setting of the light,
And then he sought a shelter for the night,
For tempest clouds rolled up from off the sea,
    With vulture flight.

Unto a farm hard by he went, to pray
A lodging ; but they asked him : 'Can you pay?'
'I have no single drachma.' They, scoffing, cried:
    'Away, away !'

Then, as they slammed the door, he turned his gaze
Upon the last, in rain expiring, rays,
And said, 'What God doth, He doeth well, I know,
        Though dark His ways.'

He was constrained to creep beneath some trees,
Through which went whistling the awaking breeze.
He lit his lamp, and set his book of prayer
        Upon his knees;

And from the book and flame the Rabbi drew
Some comfort, though the chill wind pierced through
His scanty clothing. Suddenly a gust
        The lamp outblew.

The Rabbi sighed, and shuddering drew a fold
Over his bosom to keep out the cold :
'What God hath done is well, His reasons though
        To us untold.'

And presently he heard a crash, a spring,
A howl that made the hollow forest ring.
A tiger seized his trusty dog; and Joachim
        Shrunk shuddering.

The Rabbi Joachim.

The Rabbi Joachim a deep sigh heaved :
'Of every comfort here I am bereaved ;
Yet God doth well what He hath done, in Whom
    I have believed.'

When the dawn lightened, the old man arose,
With the wet dripping from his sodden clothes,
And his teeth chattering, and his heart oppressed
    With many woes.

He tottering went towards the farm again,
Thinking, 'They now will pity my great pain.'
When lo ! he found it empty, robbed, and all
    Its inmates slain.

'Now,' said the Rabbi gravely, 'I can tell
How the Lord wrought in each thing that befell,
And know I surely that whate'er God doth,
    He doeth well.'

'Had I last night found here a home and bed,
I had this morn been lying with these dead.
The lamp-light, or the dog's bark, would the murderers
    To me have led.

'Our eyes are holden, and we cannot scan
The workings out of God's mysterious plan;
But all He doth is well, though unperceived
                        His thoughts by man.'

THE TWO SIGNS.

[FRANCISCI COSTERI *Conciones Quadr.* Col. Agrip. 1608.]

As I went past the ' Dragon ' bar,
I heard the barmaid, Susan Farr,
   Behind the taproom sighing:
' Ah me ! I lead a weary life
In midst of drunkenness and strife,
   All laughing, flirting, lying.
This is no place for me ; I pine
   Midst pewter pot and flagon :
I should do better, I should shine
As maid beneath the " Angel " sign,
   Instead of the " Green Dragon." '

Well ! I suppose that every day,
The world all over, people say,
   As long as ages wag on,

We are not in our proper sphere,
Wherein our virtues would appear;
  Here, all we do is fag on.
Now, were we left to choose our line,
We'd serve beneath the 'Angel' sign,
  And give up the 'Green Dragon.'

TURN AGAIN! (2)

[*Talmud Jerusalem*, Haggada ii. Halacha i.]

ELISHA BEN ABUJA, deeply skilled
In mysteries of science, and a Rabbi filled
With wisdom and great power of speech,
And able mightily to expound and teach,
Fell into doubt about the Holy Law,
And, from the childlike faith he had before,
From doubting little, went to doubting more.
Then broke the bonds, and cast the cords aside
That bound him in the covenant to abide,
And changed his name, and lived a Gentile life.

Then to the Rabbi, weeping, came his wife,
And said, 'When on my youth still hung the dew,
Elisha ben Abuja well I knew;

But Gentile Acher cannot be the same,
Without the father's creed, with foreign name,
I must depart from him to whence I came.'

Then drew his father nigh, with silvery head
Bent low, and bending lower, feebly said,
' I had a son, of Levi's sacred line ;
Elisha was he hight, but none of mine
Is he hight Acher. Woe ! I had a son ;
But these grey hairs bow to the grave with none
To close my eyes for me, when I am gone.'

And next his mother, with a bitter cry,
Rent out her hair, and strewed it to the sky,
Wailing : 'As these thin locks from me have sprung,
And now are torn away, and from me flung,
So is my child. He to these eyes was light
In sweet old times, now I see only night.'

His pupil Meir alone to him remained,
He by the master's learning was restrained
From leaving ; for he said : 'He teacheth well,

His equal is not found in Israel;
I eat the nut, and cast aside the shell.'
And thus, for five long years did Meir his seat
Retain, to listen at his teacher's feet;
And all this while, the Holy Law of God
Was as a lanthorn to the way he trod.
It came to pass one Sabbath day, they went
Together forth, on mutual converse bent.
The apostate Acher on a horse did ride,
With his disciple treading at his side.
And thus they fared, till Acher turned his head,
And glancing at his pupil gravely said,
' I reckon from the pacing of thy feet,
That thou hast reached the limit that is meet
To journey on the Sabbath. So refrain
From going further with me. Turn again.'

Then halted Meir, and looking in the face
Of his old master, said: 'Do thou retrace
The journey thou hast trod. Why shouldst thou roam
An exile from thy Faith, from thy True Home?
A Rabbi thou, and thou a reprobate!
Turn thee, Elisha ben Abuja! Turn again!"

'I cannot,' answered, with a spasm of pain
The apostate Acher. 'It is all too late.
As I was riding by the prostrate wall
Of Salem, in the moonlight, I heard call
A doleful voice, that to my people cried,
" Return to God ye sinners ; but abide
Thou Acher in thy sin. Thou knewest well
The way to Me, and witting, from Me fell."
Hearing that voice, I knew that I was lost,
And, in uncertainty no longer tossed,
Have burst through all restraints unto the last ;
And Hope is dead, my son—dead, like the past.'

Then cried the pupil, with distilling tear,
'O listen but one moment, master dear !
Here is a school, come with me through the door,
And hear the boys repeat the sacred lore
That they have learn'd; perchance, some word may be
Levelled with hopeful promise, ev'n at thee.'
Then Acher from his saddle leapt, awhile
Stood at the school door, with a mournful smile
Upon his lips. But Meir, he entered in,
And elder boys addressing. said, 'Begin
Recite the lessons ye this day have learned,

Each in your order, and in order cease.'
Then to the tallest of the scholars turned,
  Who spake, ' Thus saith my God, there is no peace
Unto the wicked.' *
                    So the shadow fell
Deeper upon the apostate's soul.   ' Ah! well,
Thou second scholar,' said Meir, with his rod
Pointing.   He answered, ' Master, thus saith God,
Why dost thou preach my laws, and wherefore take
My statutes in thy mouth, my law to break,
And cast my words behind thee?' †
                                  Then a moan
Escaped him standing on the threshold stone,
And Meir who heard it, with a faltering hand
  Marked out a third.   Then answered him the boy:
 . ' False tongue that speakest lies, God shall destroy
Thee from thy dwelling! from the living land
Shall root thee out!' ‡
                      A loud and bitter cry
Burst from the apostate, and with haggard eye,
And staggering feet, he turned him feebly round
To leave, and caught the doorpost,—to the ground

* Is. lvii. 21.   † Ps. l. 16.   ‡ Ps. lii. 5, 6.

Else had he fallen.   Then a little child
Came bounding up—the youngest boy—and smiled
And said : ' I know my lesson, master ; let me run
Forth to the butterflies, the flowers, the sun !'
And so to Acher, in a chanted strain,
    Repeated timidly, with bated breath:
    · He bringeth to destruction.   Then He saith,
Children of men, I bid you—TURN AGAIN!' *

Lo! when these words sank down on Acher's ears,
Forth from his heart leaped up a rush of tears,
And stretching forth his hands, as he did yearn
    For something, with a glitter on his cheek,
    Sobbing, and struggling in distress to speak,
Gasped forth at last—' I will, I will return !'

Then unto him went Meir, and whispered low :
' Elisha ben Abuja, do not go ;
"Tarry this night, and it shall be at morn,
    That He who is thy kinsman shall for thee
    Accomplish what thou wilt, and set thee free,
As the Lord liveth !   Lie thee down till dawn."' †

---

* Ps. xc. 3.   † Ruth iii. 13.

And so, Elisha, with his hands outspread
   Towards the ruined temple, fell. Into the sun—
   His task accomplished—had the scholar run,
Leaving Elisha on the threshold dead.

POPE BONIFACE VIII. (3)

Pope Boniface with folded arms was pacing in the court,
With furrowed brows and knitted lips, and spirit steeped in thought;
He scarcely gave attention to the droning of the talk
Of prelate, prince, and cardinal accompanying his walk.
They told of bitter rivalry in politics and wealth
Between the faction Ghibeline and faction of the Guelf;
How there was discord gathering, how enmity was rife,
How one side egged the other on to overt acts of strife;
How bitter words of mockery were bandied to and fro,
And each was burning with desire to smite the mortal blow,
And night and day incessantly, there sped some precious life,
Sent forth, before God summoned it, by hired assassin's knife;

How from the sacred judgment hall had justice taken
    flight,
For there was judgment only given by party, not by
    right.

A Cardinal Archbishop spoke.   'Pray Heaven from our
    land
Will root the trait'rous Ghibeline with all his murd'rous
    band,
And all his perjured judges too, and all his craft and
    stealth!'
'Out on thee!' roared a nobleman; 'the traitor is the
    Guelf.
The Guelf is ever spattering with blood the Italian soil,
Is robbing honest peasants of the object of their toil,
Is violating sacred fanes, is ruining all trade,—
Save that of the stilletto, mind! and that is rarely paid.'
'Now silence!' cried the Cardinal, with fiercely kindled
    eye;
'Back in thy throat, fell Ghibeline! I hurl that damnèd
    lie.'
'A lie! Ha, ha! Your excellence, who hatch the lies
    yourself!
If men would find rare liars, they must search the ranks
    of Guelf.'

'Now mark!' the ecclesiastic raged, 'the day will come, and must,
When Guelf shall break the Ghibeline, and stamp him to the dust,
And beat his pride to powder!'
    'So! well done, Sir Priest. *His* pride! Hurrah for Guelf humility!' the scoffing noble cried.
'I scorn you,' said the Cardinal, 'a base and beggar crew.'
'Please God,' the noble answered him, 'the Guelf shall have his due.'
'I to that supplication say my Amen gladly too!'

Then sudden stooped Pope Boniface, and without speaking, thrust
His hands along the pavement, and scrabbled up the dust.
Then rising, turned on noble and archbishop hot with ire,
His grey eye flashing lightning flakes, and launched these words of fire :
'Fond partisans, so mad with rage, I pray you, tell me whence
The Guelf and Ghibeline arose, and, when they journey hence,

To what must they return—I ask, both Ghibeline and
Guelf?
See, Ghibeline, this handful, and thou other, see thyself.
'Tis hence you sprung, to this return, when all this strife
is past.'
And in their faces, Boniface the dusty handfuls cast.

GOLDNER.

From out the hushed green forest
   Came Goldner in a dream,
      He stood a little space,
      The sun upon his face
           Did gleam.

His hair, like spun gold shining,
   His dress as silver white,
He moved, the branches parting,
   Into the full sunlight.
A fowler saw him coming
   Towards his outspread net,
His feet the dewdrops scattering
         And wet.

'Ah ha! The lad shall be
A servant unto me!'
　　The fowler thought;
　The string he drew,
　The net upflew—
　　Goldner was caught.

A year and day served Goldner,
　And then his master bade,
'Go, lad! and bring some token
　That thou hast learned the trade.'
Went Goldner to the forest,
　The sun was on his hair.
He sang, and, on the green sward
　　　　Laid the snare.
A finch with wings of silver,
　And feathers burning gold,
The lad brought, saying, 'Master,
　　　　Behold!'

'Out, wizard!' shrieked the fowler;
　'Such bird I will not see.
Away with thy enchantments
　　　　From me!'

Went Goldner to the forest,
    And wandered day and night;
The third morn from the shadows
    He walked into the light.
A gardener saw him coming,
    And pass the garden gate,
Among the sunflowers standing.
    The man thought, quite elate,
    ' The lad shall servant be
                   To me.'
    The wicket snapped :
    Goldner was trapped.

A year and day served Goldner,
    And then his master bade,
' Fetch me a stock for grafting
    From out the forest glade.
Went Goldner to the greenwood,
    And brought a brier,
    Whereon, like fire,
    Flamed a rose of gold.
                ' Master, behold !'

'Out, wizard!' shrieked the gardener,
   'Such rose I will not see;
Away with thy enchantments
               From me!'

Went Goldner to the forest,
   And wandered day and night,
The third morn from the shadows
   He walked into the light.
Before him lay an ocean
   Whimpling, translucent green,
      Over the waters lay
      A bright, quivering way
            Of sunsheen.
And gallant ships passed sailing,
With painted pennants trailing,
      And white sails flew
      Over the blue,
            Blue deep.
      Along the sandy shore
      Foam wreaths, with muffled roar,
            Did creep.

Into a boat, unheeding,
    Walked Goldner, with his eyes
Fixed in a sort of rapture
      On the skies.
The fisher cast the mooring,
    The boat stood out to sea;
'Now,' said the man, 'be servant
      To me!'
He flung the hook till evening,
    And then he Goldner bade:
'Try, lad, if thou art handy
      At the trade.'

Then cast the hook young Goldner,
    Down through the sea it flew.
He pulled, a weight was on it,
    A jewelled crown updrew.
'All hail!' the fisher shouted,
    'For he our king should be
Who the diadem should bring up
    From purple deeps of sea.'
From every ship there echoed
    The cry, 'God save the king!'
Church bells began to tinkle,
    And happy folk to sing.

And cannons puffed and thundered,
  And banners fluttered high,
And rockets started, powdering
  With fire the evening sky.

Upon the prow stood Goldner,
  The crown upon his hair,
Dripping with salt sea-water,
  His gold locks in the air
            Flowing.
  The west was all ablaze,
  Upon the sun, his gaze
  Rested silent and in amaze,
            And his face glowing.

THE LITTLE SCHOLAR. (4)

[CÆSARIUS HEISTERBACHENSIS, lib. ii. c. 10.]

THERE went a little scholar
    With slow and lagging feet
Towards the great church portal
    That opened on the street.

Without, the sun was shining;
    Within, the air was dim;
He caught a waft of incense,
    A dying note of hymn.

He drew the crimson curtain,
    And cast a look inside,
To where the sunbeam lightened
    The form of Him who died,
Between Saint John and Mary
    On roodloft crucified.

The Little Scholar.

The curtain fell behind him,
　　He stood a little while,
Then signed him with the water,
　　And rambled down the aisle,

Behind a great brown pillar
　　The scholar took his stand,
And trifled with the ribbon
　　Of the satchel in his hand.

His little breast was beating,
　　His blue eyes brimming o'er;
Like April rains, his tears
　　Fell spangling on the floor.

An aged priest was passing;
　　He noticed him, and said,
'Why, little one, this weeping,
　　This heavy hanging head?'

'My father, O my father!
　　I've sinned,' said the child;
'And have no rest of conscience
　　Till I am reconciled.

The Little Scholar.

Then list to my confession'—
    He louted on his knee—
'The weight of my transgression
    Weighs heavily on me.'

But then a burst of weeping
    And sobs his utterance broke,
The priest could not distinguish
    A single word he spoke.

In vain were all his efforts,
    For wildly tossed his breast,
He could not still the tumult,
    With hands upon it pressed.

Then said the pastor gently,
    'You have a little slate;
Write on it the confession
    You are powerless to relate.'

The child his satchel opened,
    And strove his sins to note,
But still the tear-drops dribbled,
    As busily he wrote.

Now when the tale was finished,
    He held it to the priest
With sigh, as from the burden
    He felt himself released.

The old man raised the tablet
    To read what there was set,
But could not, for the writing
    Was blotted with the wet.

Then turned the aged confessor
    Towards the kneeling boy,
With countenance all shining
    In rapture of pure joy.

'Depart in peace, forgiven,
    Away with doubting fears!
Thy sins have all been cancelled
    By the torrent of thy tears.'

THORKELL-MANI.

[' Thorkell-Máni, the President, son of Thorstein, was a heathen, living a good life as far as his light went. In his death-sickness, he had himself brought out into the sunshine, and committed himself into the hands of the God who made the sun. He had also lived a clean life, better than many a Christian who knew better.'—*Landnáma Bok*, i. c. 9.]

I AM dying, O my children ! come around my bed,
My feet are cold as ashes, heavy is my head ;
You see me powerless lying,—I, who was of old
The scourge of evil-doers, Thorkell stout and bold.
I cannot mount my war-horse, now I cannot wield
My great blue sword there hanging, rusting by my shield.
Sons, look at these white fingers, quivering and weak,
Without the power a slender sammet thread to break.
My sons ! I have been asking whither I shall go,
When this old body withers. Sons ! I do not know.
There is a tale of Odin, sitting in Valhall,
Who to a banquet summons those in strife who fall,

To drink and to be drunken, then to rise and fight,
To wound and to be wounded, be smitten and to smite.
But when a man is drawing to the close of life,
He yearns for something other than eternal strife;
And it is slender comfort, when he craveth peace,
To hear of war and bloodshed that shall never cease.
But He the sun who fashioned in the skies above,
And who the moon suspended, surely must be Love.
Now therefore, O my children, do this thing I ask,
Transport me through the doorway in the sun to bask.
Upon that bright globe gliding through the deep blue sky,
Gazing—thus, and only thus, in comfort can I die.
For chambered here in darkness, on my doubts I brood,
But in the mellow sunlight I feel that God is good.
A God to mortals tender, the very Fount of light—
Not Odin, whose whole glory is to booze and fight.
What prospect opens to me, when gathered to the dust?
I feel I the Creator of the sun may trust.
He lays that lamp of beauty in a western bed,
And every morn it liveth, rising from the dead.
And if the sun, a creature, can arouse the grain,
That like a corpse entombed, long time in earth hath lain
Then, surely, the Creator—wherefore be afraid?—
Will care for man, the noblest creature He hath made.

Away with Thorr and Odin. To Him who made the sun
I yield the life He gave me, which now seemeth done.
Then through the doorway bear me, lads, that I may die
With sunlight falling round me, my face towards the sky.

A PARABLE.

A youth caught up an aged pilgrim on the way
Of life, and to him said : ' My father, tell me, pray,
Where Paradise may lie, that I may thither speed.'
The old man halted, and thus answered him : ' Indeed.
The road I know full well, my son : look on before—
Yonder is Paradise, and yonder is the door.'
Thereat, off sped the youth, with bounding step to fly
Towards the portal.
     But loud after him did cry
The old man. ' Not so; Paradise must entered be
On crutches, and with gouty feet, as done by me.'

BLIND AUSTIN. (5)

IN a lonely hut, a shepherd
    Lived to God with tranquil mind,
Cherished by an only daughter,
    And the aged man was blind.

Five and twenty years had vanished
    Since God shut the shepherd's eyes,
Since he saw the waving meadows,
    And the ever-changing skies.

Never had his eyes, unclouded,
    Looked upon the simple child,
That in tender growing beauty
    On the old man beamed and smiled.

But with open heart, undarkened,
    Gently would poor Austin say,
'God, who pleased to give me vision,
    At His pleasure took away.'

Hour by hour he tarried, kneeling,
    With dark orbs upon the sky,
Wrapped in silent contemplation,
    Praying, praising inwardly.

When the evening shadows gathered,
    And the weary world was calm,
At his casement lingered Austin,
    Singing low his vesper psalm.

Said the maiden, one day, 'Father!
    I have heard, on yonder hill
Is a chapel for poor pilgrims,
    Where is healed each mortal ill.

'There the deaf recover hearing,
    There the lame foot leapeth light,
There the feeble gather vigour,
    There the blind regain their sight.'

Hearing this, the old man trembled:
'Oh, that sight were given me!
That the glory of creation
  Once again these eyes might see.

'See the yellow sun of summer,
  And the moon and stars of night,
See the ruddy firelight flicker,
  See again all gladdening light.

'See the hawthorn in the hedges,
  And the daisy at my feet,
See the scarlet poppies winking
  In the waving amber wheat.

'See my little crumbling cottage,
  And the misty smoke upcurl;
See *thee*, whom I clasp and cling to—
  Thee, my own dear little girl!'

Through the weary night he wakened,
  Tossing fevered on his bed,
Sighing, 'Oh, were light of heaven
  On these darkened eyeballs shed!'

Blind Austin.

Forth he sped at early morning ;
   To that shrine his way to grope.
Heeding not the toilsome journey,
   In the eagerness of hope.

Lo! he kneels in Mary's chapel,
   Weary, wayworn, faint, footsore,
With his tremulous arms expanded,
   Praying on the sacred floor.

' Holy Saviour, only succour!
   Ope my eyes that I may see!
Gentle Mary, Virgin Mother!
   In compassion pray for me!'

Then—a sudden cry of rapture,
   And a glad ecstatic thrill—
Flowed the light whence long excluded,
   Seeming all his frame to fill.

Now he saw the rustic altar,
   With its flowers and candles six.
And the ruby star which glimmered
   Wavering before the pyx.

Now beheld the little maiden,
    Kneeling in a golden beam,
Tranced in wondering devotion,
    Like an angel in a dream.

Now beheld the throng of pilgrims
    Gathered in Our Lady's shrine,
Now beheld the sun of summer
    Through the western window shine.

Saw a glimmer through the doorway
    Of a vaporous azure plain,
Saw the swallows, in the sunlight,
    Skimming low before the rain.

Saw a bush of flowering elder,
    And dog-daisies in its shade,
Tufted meadow-sweet entangled
    In a blushing wild-rose braid.

Saw a distant sheet of water,
    Flashing like a fallen sun;
Saw the winking of the ripples
    Where the mountain torrents run.

Saw the peaceful arch of heaven,
    With a cloudlet on the blue,
Like a white bird winging homeward
    With its feathers drenched in dew.

Then old Austin sought to gather
    All his thoughts for fervent praise;
But, alas! their chains are shattered,
    Every thought in freedom strays.

Austin sought his heart to quicken
    For the solemn act of prayer;
But from earth's absorbing beauties
    Not a moment can it spare;
And attention is distracted,
    Straying here and straying there.

Cried the shepherd, 'O my Saviour!'—
    With a sudden grief oppressed—
'Be Thy will, not mine, accomplished;
    Give me what Thou deemest best.'

Then once more the clouds descended,
    And the eyes again waxed dark;
All the splendour of the sunlight
    Faded to a dying spark.

But the closèd heart expanded,
  Like the flower that blooms at night.
Whilst, as Philomel, the spirit
  Chanted to the waning light.

'Shut my eyes,' the old man whispered;
  'Close to earth's distracting sight,
Till the spirit breaks its fetters,
  Speeding heavenward its flight.
Then to open to the glory
  Of Thine uncreated light!'

LANCELOT.

SWIFT and dark set in the night,
Yet, in the north, a pallid light,
As a glimmering thread of white,
    Lay, blotted with black trees.
Lancelot at the church door stood,
Holding with his hands to the wood,
Muffling his features in his hood,
    Aghast, and with quaking knees.

Wherefore aghast, he could not tell.
Then rang out the compline bell,
But it sounded like a knell
    In that evening hot and still.
A bat came wheeling by,
Dashing out of the dark sky,
And diving in presently.
    Far off, on a low hill,

Sudden, flashed out a spark ;
A dog began to bark ;
The light vanished, and all was dark,
    Save that shimmer in the north.
A wild-fowl flight o'erhead,
Northward whistling sped,
By wondrous instinct led,
    Whilst Lancelot looked forth.

Up leaped a silvery ray,
Like the dawning of new day,
To the northward far away,
    And tremulously danced.
Then another beam arose,
In fitful throbs and throes,
Of the colour of the rose,
    As Lancelot gazed entranced.

A mighty shining bow,
Of deep carnation glow,
O'er the vault began to grow,
    And fall to flakes of fire ;

Then drop, a glittering rain,
Or gathering again
In patches of red stain,
    Waste away, and then expire.

Now swept a fog of blight
Betwixt Lancelot and the light,
Obscuring for a while all sight
    In a glowing furnace-blast;—
Whereat the shadowy trees
Writhed as in agonies,
Or shivered, till the breeze
    And the cloud were past.

On Lancelot's ear a tread
Sounded, heavy, measured,
And Lancelot would have fled,
    But was paralysed with fear.
Like a memory, deemed slain,
Of past guilt, which throbs again
In pulses of dull pain,
    Came the tread upon his ear.

Now, stalking past the door,
Lancelot a figure saw
He had never seen before,
    Like a vision of the dead.
And as it nearer drew,
He marked the yellow hue
Of the face, and locks which blew
    Tangled around the head.
In a flapping orange vest,
It strode.—It was the Pest.
It smote Lancelot on the breast,
    And Lancelot's spirit fled.

THE SWALLOWS OF CITEAUX. (6)

[Cæsarius Heisterbachensis, lib. x. c. 58.]

Under eaves, against the towers,
All the spring, their muddy bowers
    Swallows build about Citeaux.
Round the chapter house and hall,
From the dawn to evenfall,
    They are fluttering to and fro

On their never-flagging wing.
With the psalms the brethren sing
    Blends their loud incessant cry ;
In and out the plastered nest,
Never taking thought of rest,
    Chattering these swallows fly.

They distract the monk who reads,
Him as well who tells his beads,
    Him who writes his chronicle :
In the cloister old and grey
They are jubilant and gay,
    In the very church as well.

On the dormitory beds,
In refectory o'er the heads—
    At the windows rich with paint,
Ever dashing,—in and out
With the maddest, noisiest rout,
    As would surely vex a saint.

To the abbot then complain
Pious monks :—' Shall these remain
    To disturb us at our prayers?
Bid us nests and eggs destroy,
Then the birds will not annoy
    Any more our deafened ears.'

Quoth the abbot, smiling—' Say,
Have not we, too, homes of clay,
    Quite as fragile, not more fair?
Brothers, and shall we resolve
Their tabernacles to dissolve,
    Asking God our own to spare?'

Not another word of blame,
But they turned away in shame,
    So the little birds had peace,
And the parapets among
Built and laid, and hatched their young,
    Making wonderful increase.

When declined the autumn sun,
When the yellow harvest done,
    Sat the swallows in a row
On the ridging of the roof,
Patiently, as in behoof
    Of a licence ere they'd go.

The Swallows of Citeaux.

Forth from out the western door
Came the abbot ; him before
    Went a brother with his crook,
And a boy a bell who rung
And a silver censer swung,
    Whilst another bore the book.

Then the abbot raised his hand,
Looking to the swallow band,
    Saying, ' Ite, missa est !
Christian birds, depart in peace,
As your cares of summer cease,
    Swallows, enter on your rest.

' Now the winter snow must fall,
Wrapping earth as with a pall,
    And the stormy winds arise.
Go to distant lands where glow
Deathless suns, where falls not snow
    From the ever azure skies.

The Swallows of Citeaux.

'Go ! dear heralds of the road,
  To the sweet unknown abode
     In the verdant Blessed Isles,
  Whither we shall speed some day,
  Leaving crumbling homes of clay
     For the land where summer smiles.

'Go in peace ! your hours have run ;
  Go, the day of work is done ;
     Go in peace, my sons !' he said.
  Then the swallows spread the wing,
  Making all the welkin ring
     With their cry, and southward sped.

POOR ROBIN.

[MEFFRET, *Hortulus Reginæ.* Norimb. 1487.]

Robin the cobbler, blithe and gay,
Fiddled at night time, cobbled at day;
Busily worked till the curfew rang,
Then caught up his bow and fiddled and sang.
Robin lived under a marble stair
That led to a terrace broad and fair
Adorned with exotics bright and rare,
Where, every evening, taking the air,
A nobleman walked with brow depressed,
And within his bosom a sea of unrest;
Trembling now at the frown of the king,
Lest titles and honours should spread their wing;
Now at the fate of a suit at court,
Then at some insult to be out-fought;
But oh! for the cares unreckoned that rolled
From that plentiful source,—the lust of gold.

Poor Robin.

The nobleman watched the declining sun,
Day with its business and cares was done ;
And now, for the vigorous sons of toil,
To the wearied spirits came glad recoil.
But for such as the nobleman came no rest
As the sun went down in the scarlet west ;
For rest is none from ambition's strain,
None for the heart where pride holds reign,
None for the breast filled with greed of gain.
Then sudden he heard the tremulous string
Robin's sweet carol accompanying ;
Unreckoned the hours that glided by,
As Robin sat twittering cheerily,
With the moon going up in the darkling sky.

'Now this is strange,' the nobleman said,
'That a poor man labouring for his bread,
With a crust to eat, and a strawstrewn bed,
Should be so jubilant, free from sorrow,
Without a care or thought of the morrow.
The secret of having light heart, if found,
Cheap would I count at a thousand pound.'

When Robin was out at a job one day,
The nobleman hid a gold bag in the hay

Of the cobbler's pillow, and hasted away.
That night, as its wont, the curfew rang,
But Robin the cobbler nor fiddled nor sang,
For in turning his pillow his glad eyes fell
On the purse with a wonder unspeakable.

Now silent and musing he sat till late,
His heart oppressed with a leaden weight,
His mind revolving where to conceal
The treasure, where none might find and steal.
Cautiously locking and bolting his door,
He buried the purse underneath the floor,
Then over it strewed his litter of straw.
Little he slept, waking often in fear,
Imagining burglars drawing near,
Slumber unbroken seemed fled for e'er.

Night after night the nobleman strode
The terrace above poor Robin's abode;
But hushed was the voice of the cobbler now,
And laid aside were the fiddle and bow.

Then the nobleman stood before Robin's stall,
And said, 'By accident I let fall
A purse of gold, through a chink in the wall,

Into thy cell, to thy straw it rolled;
Now have I come to reclaim my gold.'
Then the poor cobbler upraised a board,
Extracted the purse and the prize restored.
And scarce had the nobleman turned away,
Ere he heard the fiddler begin to play,
And he had not reached his terrace again
Ere the voice was chirping a jocund strain.

THE OLIVE TREE.

Said an ancient hermit, bending
    Half in prayer upon his knee,
'Oil I need for midnight watching,
    I desire an olive tree.'

Then he took a tender sapling,
    Planted it before his cave,
Spread his trembling hands above it,
    As his benison he gave.

But he thought, the rain it needeth,
    That the root may drink and swell:
'God! I pray Thee send thy showers!'
    So a gentle shower fell.

'Lord! I ask for beams of summer,
    Cherishing this little child.'
Then the dripping clouds divided,
    And the sun looked down and smiled.

' Send it frost to brace its tissues,
    O my God!' the hermit cried.
Then the plant was bright and hoary,
    But at evensong it died.

Went the hermit to a brother
    Sitting in his rocky cell:
'Thou an olive-tree possessest;
    How is this, my brother, tell?

' I have planted one, and prayed,
    Now for sunshine, now for rain;
God hath granted each petition,
    Yet my olive-tree hath slain!'

Said the other, ' I intrusted
    To its God my little tree;
He who made knew what it needed
    Better than a man like me.

'Laid I on Him no condition,
　　Fixed not ways and means ; so I
Wonder not my olive thriveth,
　　Whilst thy olive tree did die.'

BISHOP BENNO AND THE FROGS.

 At the closing of the day
Bishop Benno took his way,
  With his book beneath his arm,
Through the meadows for a stroll,
The disturbance of his soul
  To reduce again to calm.

Walking by a marish bank,
Where the yellow iris lank
  Shot its bluish, bending sheath.
Whilst upon the surface, light
Floated chalices of white,
  Anchored to the slime beneath.

Bishop Benno and the Frogs.

Where about the margin grew
Clusters of celestial blue,
    And the bog-bean speckled pink,
And the mare-tails with their spines
Stood and shook in shadowy lines
    Wavering along the brink.

Clearly from the minster tower
Tolling at the twilight hour,
    Salutation spoke the bell.*
Then the Bishop slowly took,
And unclasped his Office book,
    To recite his Canticle.

Walking in the meadow grass,
By the water still as glass,
    He could lift his voice and pray;
Reading in his Breviary,
Repeating Benedicite
    As he wended on his way

* The Angelus rings at noon and sunset.

Perched on broken bulrush shaft,
Crouched on lily's leafy raft,
    Sitting in a row on logs,
Squatted on each muddy ledge,
Sentineled along the edge
    Of the water, were the frogs;

With their voices very shrill,
In a loud prolonging thrill,
    Half a chirrup, half a cry;
Every little gullet shakes,
As its clamour from it breaks,
    Deafening the passer-by.

Bishop Benno halting stood,
Looking at them in a mood
    Discontented; he could find,
Saying the Three Children's Song,
As he paced the bank along,
    No tranquillity of mind.

'O ye frogs! when Bishops praise
God, ye should amend your ways,
And be quiet for a while.'
Thus he spake, and at the word
They were silent, naught was heard.
He continued, with a smile :

'All ye green things on the earth,
Bless the Lord who gave you birth,
And for ever magnify.
All ye fountains that are poured
From your sources, praise the Lord,
And for ever magnify.

'All ye seas and floods that roll,
Praise the Lord, from pole to pole,
And for ever magnify.
All ye teeming things that dwell
In the waters, praise as well,
And for ever magnify.'

Sudden Benno stopped. A flame
Started to his brow, in shame,
 As he did within debate.
'What! doth the Creator love
Praises from the things that move,
 And from things inanimate?

'Fie upon me! Am I sure
My intent is half as pure,
 Praises as acceptable,
As the strain, though loud and harsh,
Of these dwellers in the marsh?
 What am I, that I can tell?'

Turning to the swamp, he cried:
'Sitters by the water-side,
 Do not ye your hymns forego.
I release you from the ban,
Praise the God of Frog and Man—
 Cantate fratres Domino.'

THE UNIVERSAL MOTHER.

[*Pirke Rabbi Elieser*, 11.]

WHEN by the hand of God man was created,
He took the dust of earth from every quarter—
From east and west, and from the north and south—
That wheresoever man might wander forth,
He should be still at home; and, when a-dying,
On some far distant western shore, and seeking
A shelter in the bosom of the Mother,
The earth might not refuse to clasp him, saying,
' My offspring art thou not, O roving Eastern.'

Wherever now the foot of Man shall bear him,
Wherever by the final call o'ertaken,
He is no stranger reckoned, or an outcast,
But hears exclaim the Universal Mother,
' Come, child of mine, and slumber in my bosom.'

THE LOAN.

[*Midrash Jalkut*, iii. p. 165.]

The Rabbi Meir,
A black cap on his white hair,
And him before
Unfurled the great book of the Law,
Sat in the school and taught.
Many a wingèd thought
Flew from his lips, and brought
Fire and enlightenment
Unto the scholars bent
Diligently at their writing.
And all the while he was inditing,
His soul was near to God
Above the dull earth that he trod.
And as the lark doth sing

The Loan.

High up and quivering
In the blue, on heavenward wing,
But ever its breast
Keepeth above its nest,
And singing it doth not roam
Beyond hearing of its home,
So the Rabbi, however high he soared
    In his teaching, or praying, sung
Close to the ear of his LORD,
    Yet ever above his home, his wife and young.

Slowly there stole the gloom
Of evening into the room,
Then he rose and shut the book,
And casting about a look,
Said, with a wave
Of the hand: 'God gave
The light, and hath taken away.
With the Lord begun,
With the Lord run,
With the Lord done,
Is the day.'
Then his way
Homeward cheerfully he took.

The Loan.

In the little house, sedate,
For her husband did await
Beruiah. And for her lord
She had laid the supper on the board.
And a lamp was lighted up,
By the which he might sup.
He kissed her upon the brow,
And spake to her gently: 'How
Are the lads to-day?
Tell me, Beruiah, pray.'
There glittered on her cheek
Two jewels, ere she could speak
And answer, 'They are well.
Sit you and eat your supper, whilst I tell
What to me befell;
And assure me in what way
You think it had been best
That I had acted.' Thus addressed,
He sat him at his meal,
And began to eat: 'Reveal
Thy case,' he said. 'Yet tell me, I pray,
First—where are my boys to-day?'
Then suddenly she said,
With an averted head:

'Many years are flown
Since one a very precious loan
Entrusted to my care, until he came
That treasure to reclaim.'
The Rabbi spoke : 'Of old
Tobit confided his gold
To Raguel
At Ecbatane. Well,
What further ?—But say,
Where are my lads, I pray ?'

'For many years that store
I jealously watched o'er.
Do you think, my lord, that loan
In fourteen years would become my own ?'
Then, with a glance of blame,
He answered, as he shook his head : 'For shame,
Wife of my bosom ! It were not thine
Should forty years upon thee shine,
And the owner not return
To demand it. Beruiah, learn
Not to covet.'
                    Then he paused, and said,
Moving the lamp : 'Thine eyes are red,

The Loan.

Beruiah: wherefore?'
      But she broke
In on his question, and thus spoke:
'To-day there came
To the door the same
One who had lent the treasure,
And he said, "It is my pleasure
To have the loan restor'd."
What do you think, my lord?
Should I have withheld it, Meir?'
At his wife with astonished stare
Looked the Rabbi. 'O my wife!
Light of my eyes, and glory of my life!
Why ask this question?'
      Then he said,
As his eyes wandered towards the bed:
'Why is the sheet,
Usually smooth and neat,
Lifted into many a fold and pleat?'
But she asked: 'Should I repine
At surrendering what was not mine
To him who claimed it?'
     'It was a trust,
Wife of my bosom! What do you ask?— Repine

What! do you lust
To keep what is not thine?'
And once again:
'Where are my boys?'
                      She took him by the hand,
Whilst o'er her features ran a thrill of pain,
And brought him to the bed, and bid him stand
There, as she touched the sheet, and said:
'The Lord who gave hath taken. They are dead.'
Softly she raised
The sheet; and with awe
The Rabbi his children saw
In the soft twilight
Lying silent, and still and white;
And he said, 'Praised
  Be the Name of the Lord.
My wife and I are content
That the goodly loan to us lent
  Should be restored.'

DOCTOR FAUSTUS.

GREAT DOCTOR FAUSTUS to the Fiend had sold
His soul and body for large store of gold.
And now, a wonderment and longing came
To see the place in everlasting flame
That he should occupy, when was unfurled
Upon his gaze the unseen world,
Where he must linger out, without repeal,
An endless waste of being, 'neath the seal
Of righteous doom.
                A mighty spell he wrought.
And to his side the evil angel brought,
And then commanded him : ' I bid you bear
Me on thy pinions through the murky air,
Unto the region whither thou art cast,
And show me where, when this brief life is past.
I shall be tortured.'

      Then said Satan : 'Seat
Thyself upon my back, and let thy feet
Depend on either side. Be not afraid,
Thy time is not yet come.'
        Faustus obeyed.
The Evil One upsprang from earth, and flew
Whither I know not; but there fell a shade
That gradually blotted out the blue
Of heaven, and all grew ghastly, blear, and **dark**;
The sun diminished to a flickering spark,
And then expired in smoke, and there was none
Of light, when they had lost the sun.
A long while traversed they the awful gloom,
That stagnant lay, in which did nothing loom
Upon the Doctor's eyes, nor sound whate'er
Vibrate upon the turgid air,
Except the striding of the angel's wings,
And mutter of the air's low quiverings.
Incontinent, the Doctor Faustus broke
The silence, with a sudden word that woke
No answering echo, had no ring, but fell
Apart at every syllable.
And dropped into oblivion in their wake;
Nor did the evil angel answer make.

Then, for a second, with a batlike shriek
Of parted air, and labouring creak
Of beating pinions, in the dark went by
A spirit from the abyss, to mortal eye
Unseen.
   How long the time in passing through
The murky darkness, Faustus never knew;
For, in that gloom, there was no change to tell
Of time—but unendurable
Whether a second or a century,
For there eternity had ceased to be
Articulate. Upon the doctor's breast
The darkness weighed, and with the weight oppress'd
The horror of that life-divested air
Seemed to be palpable despair.

At once the veil was riven over head,
And through the abyss a beam of light was shed,
That travelled down, a solid silver flake
That on no object fell, or lit to break,
Save Faustus, who looked up with eager start,
And saw the blackened heavens part,
And for one instant, only one, disclose
The Paradise where happy souls repose—

Sudden saw the Heavenly City
    Built of bright and burnished gold,
Lying in transcendent beauty,
    Stored with treasures all untold.

In the midst of that fair city
    Christ was throned upon His seat,
Whilst the angels swung their censers
    In a ring about His feet.

From that throne a river issued,
    Clear as crystal, passing bright,
Traversing the Holy City
    Like a sudden beam of light.

Where it watered leafy Eden,
    Rolling over silver sands,
Sat the angels softly chiming
    On the harps between their hands.

There he saw the meadows dewy
    Spread with lilies wondrous fair;
Thousand, thousand were the colours
    Of the waving flowers there.

Dr. Faustus.

There were forests ever blooming
    As our orchards here in May;
There were gardens never fading,
    Which eternally are gay.

There he saw the red carnation,
    Rose and honeysuckle twine;
There along the river edges
    Saw the golden jonquil shine;

There the water-lilies lying,
    Open on the sea of glass,
There the yellow crocus glimmer
    Like a flame amidst the grass.

Caught a fragment of the music,
    Loud as thunder, of the song
Of the Seraph, and the Elder,
    And the great redeemèd throng.

Again on earth as Doctor Faustus stood,
With wrinkled brow, in an abstracted mood,
To him came Wagner, eager, and on fire
With curiosity, to enquire

What had been seen below. 'Master,' he said,
'Describe to me the sort of bed
On which you will be stretched when life is o'er:
What place in Hell is there for thee in store?'

Then Faustus answered, thickly speaking: 'Oh!
I cannot tell, my friend; I do not know.
I may have seen it, but I little wot,
Whether I did behold the place or not.'
Then, as his bosom with convulsion tossed,
He said: 'Remembered only what is lost;
Seen for one second the celestial shore,
I can remember nothing more—
That I recall; all else is quite forgot.'

THE WIFE'S TREASURE.

[*Midrash Yalkut*, cap. 17.]

AT Sidon lived a husband with his wife
For ten long years, leading a tranquil life,
With but a single grief—they had no child.
And, to his barren lot unreconciled,
The man upon it brooded. Then he bent
His steps to Rabbi Simeon, with intent
To be divorced; and to the woman's tears
He steeled his heart, and said : 'Ten happy years
In peacefulness with thee, true heart, I spent ;
Stanch wert thou ever, nor a word to smart
Escaped thy lips. And now, before we part,
I will accord the treasure thou dost find
In thy old home best suited to thy mind.
Take it; whate'er it be, it shall be thine,
To solace thee when thou no more art mine.'

Then said the Rabbi Simeon: 'O ye pair!
Before ye separate, a feast prepare,
And pledge each other in the ruddy wine;
Then the feast ended, woman, unto thine
Own father's house do thou repair.'
That very night the supper board was spread,
According to the law; one seated at the head,
The other at the bottom.   To the brim
The woman filled the bowl and passed it him.
And then he pledged her, and she filled again,
And he the goblet to his wife did drain
Once more, with many wishes good and fair.
But she the generous liquor did not spare,
Until he fell into a drunken sleep,
With head upon the table, heavy and deep.
And thus concluded the farewell carouse.
So then, she took him up with gentle care
Upon her shoulder, and her husband bare,
Nodding and drowsing, to her father's house.
And laid him on the bed.
      At peep of day
He started up and said: 'Woman! I pray,
Tell me, where am I?'

     She to him replied :
'You promised me that nought should be denied
To me of what I valued. I could find,
In all thy house, thee only to my mind,
And I have borne thee hither ; now, I trow
That thou art mine ; I will not let thee go.
When I was thine, thou wouldst be quit of me ;
Now thou art mine, and I will treasure thee !'

THE ARMS OF MAYENCE.

ALL the bells of Mainz were rung,
A Processional was sung
    By the clergy in the street,
Going to invest in pall*
Their Archbishop, and install,
    In the great cathedral seat.

There was gathered dense a throng
All the narrow way along,
    Full of happy wonderment,
As the acolytes upthrew
Fragrant wreaths of misty blue,
    And the banners past them went.

---

* The pall of white wool was the badge of an Archbishop.

Willigis the wheelwright's son,
Chosen for the vacant throne,
    In episcopal array,
Followed 'neath an awning spread,
Borne by deacons, o'er his head,
    And with flaunting feathers gay.

Whilst proceeding, he could trace
Mockery on every face
    That was turned to Willigis.
And there fell upon his ear
Many a cruel jibe and jeer,
    And occasionally a hiss.

Then a laugh among the crowd,
Low at first, but waxing loud.
    Slightly turning on his heels,
He beheld, on hands and feet,
Urchins running down the street,
    Nimbly, as revolving wheels.

All the way on either side
Bishop Willigis descried,
 On each shoring, plank and balk,
To the people's great delight,
By some jester,—cartwheels white
 Rudely drawn in common chalk.

Though they watch him, none discern
Colour in his cheek to burn,
 Or a sparkle in his eye.
With his hands upon his breast,
And his humble head depress'd,
 Calmly Willigis went by.

As he pondered in his stall
At the minster, on the wall
 He perceived, upon a crank,
Hung a shield, whereon should be
The Archbishop's blazonry,
 But the surface was left blank.

Then a painter in the aisle
Beck'ning to him with a smile,
    Bending low, he whispered:
'If a Bishop arms have none,
May he then select his own?'
    'Yes, he may,' was answered.

'Fetch thy brush and paint, my son!
When the installation done.
    Decorate for me that shield;
That I ever bear in sight
My achievement—Cartwheel white
    Figured on a ruby field.

'Paint it over porch and door
Where my predecessor bore
    Haughty blazon. That, among
Those I meet of noble birth—
Princes, mighty of the earth—
    I forget not whence I sprung!'

If you visit aged Mayence,
Then, I pray you, give a glance
    At the blazon that it bears.
You will find that it has borne
The White Cartwheel it did scorn,
    Proudly for eight hundred years.

You will read in ancient book
How the grateful city took
    For its badge the wheelwright's sign,
In thanksgiving for his reign—
One of love, and peace, and gain—
    Brightest of the sacred line.

THE MASS FOR THE DEAD.

A LEGEND OF MESSINA.

ALL day unflagging in his stall
   Sat Hildebrand the priest, and heard
Confessions made, and over all
   He uttered the absolving word.

But as the light of garish day
Passed with the setting sun away,
A heaviness and languor stole
All unperceived upon his soul.

Full oft at the confided sin
   The tender-hearted priest had wept ;
Now wearied, as the dusk set in,
   He leaned him back and slept.

Nor woke he to the vesper bell,
Nor heard the organ's solemn swell,
And only turned upon his seat
At tramp of the retreating feet.

Heard not the verger's closing call,
   Nor chiming of the transept clock,
Heard not the doors together fall,
   Nor noisy key turn'd in the lock.

And as the night hours glided by,
And Charles's wain wheeled in the sky,
Priest Hildebrand slept heavily.

Now first a spark, and then a flame,
Like an uplighted beacon, came;
And next a streak of silver light
That smote along the vaulted height,
As the moon in her last quarter
Rose out of the eastern water.

Sudden pealed the watchman's blast
When the noon of night was past,

The Mass for the Dead.

And the echoes clung awhile
To the ribbing of the aisle.
Still did the slumb'ring pastor rest
With grey head nodding on his breast.

And thus the night hours glided by,
As Charles's Wain wheeled in the sky,
And Hildebrand slept heavily.

The presses and misereres of oak
Warped and snapped ; each noisy stroke
Of the minster clock, though clear,
Unheeded fell upon the ear.
A sea-breeze rose, and idly strayed
Over the window glass, and played
Faint pipings where it found a rent,
Or sung about the battlement.

A click—a rush of whirring wheels,
The hammer of the old clock reels,
And strikes one stroke upon the gong,
With long-drawn after undersong.

Then, suddenly, the sleep-bands broke,
And Hildebrand the priest awoke,
And conscious instantly, he gave
One stride, and found him in the nave.
Then started, with a sense of awe,
As he the whole interior saw
With light illum'd, but wan and faint,
By which each shrine and sculptured saint,
Each marble shaft and fretted niche,
The moulded arch, the tracery rich,
The brazen eagle in the choir,
The bishop's throne with gilded spire,
Stood out as clear as on a day
When clouds obscure the solar ray.
The altar tapers were alight,
Chalice and paten glimmered bright,
The service book was opened wide,
Wafers and cruets were at one side,
And, on the rail, in meet array,
Alb, amice, stole and vestment lay.
And one knelt on the altar stair
As server, hushed, immersed in prayer,
In convent garb, and with feet bare.

The Mass for the Dead.

Now with a shrinking and surprise,
And scarcely crediting his eyes,
The priest discerned the whitened bone
Of feet, where skin and flesh was none.

With quivering knees, and throbbing blood,
And chattering teeth, the roused man stood;
Whilst each vibration of the clock
Beat on his pulse with liveliest shock.

Up rose the monk—and his bones ground
As he arose—and turned him round,
And spread abroad his wasted hands,
As doth the celebrant who stands,
And makes the dread adorèd sign,
To close the mysteries divine.

Sudden a voice the silence broke,
With words articulate, and spoke
   From underneath the drooping cowl.
As clear as ring of sanctus bell,
Hildebrand heard each syllable:
   'Who mass will offer for my soul?'

'I will!' cried Hildebrand, and strode
Towards the altar of his God.

And so that night it came to pass
A priest intoned the holy mass,
In that cathedral, for one dead,
Whose soul unshriven suffered;
And all the while he prayed, he felt
That a dead man behind him knelt.
But on the face he dared not look
Of him who served the holy book,
The cruets, and the sacred bread,
With serge cowl covering his head.

Now, when his office was complete,
He marked the monk upon his knees,
Who muttered, as winds sound in trees,
  And, with dead hands, held fast his feet
Who said:
          'What years of bitter pain
My soul in Purgatory hath lain,
And panted for release in vain!
Beneath yon slab my body lies,
No loving fingers closed my eyes,

But, wrestling in death's agonies,
Alone I breathed my parting sighs.
Yonder was an unguarded well,*
Down which, by fatal chance, I fell;
And where I was no mortal knew,
For no man thence the water drew;
And through the town the rumour spread
That from my cloister I had fled.
Thus for my soul no mass was said,
Nor was my body burièd.
And, as the well was used no more,
As time passed, it was covered o'er.
But nightly for two hundred years
Here have I cried aloud with tears,
And none have heard my wail till now,
Or answered to my prayer, but thou.
Priest Hildebrand! God's blessing light
Upon thee for thy deed this night.
I would repay, but power have none—
Save this, that ere thy sands are run,
  I will appear again.'

---

* Several foreign cathedrals have wells within the building. That in Strasbourg has been only lately closed.

And as he spake, a pallid ray,
The harbinger of coming day,
  Smote through the eastern pane.
Then first, enabled by God's grace,
The priest looked on the dead man's face,
That turned towards the Crucified
As in a rapture, glorified.
And with great reverence, Hildebrand,
Extending o'er the monk his hand,
Traced upon the ashy brow
  And the uplifted head
The sacred sign which angels know
And devils fear. So, saying 'Peace!'
The monk responded, 'With release,'
  And vanishèd.

THE LUCK FLOWER.

[*Curious Myths of the Middle Ages*, Series II. p. 137, 1868.]

A MEADOW tremulous with dew,
A lifted firmament all blue,
And bushes shedding many a tear—
But all of joy—in the morning clear;
Bending bladed grasses fret
In the light wind, dripping wet;
Buttercups adorn the floor
With their goblets brimming o'er;
Purple orchis lines the hedge;
Marigold gleams in the sedge;
Robin shakes his jaunty tatters,
And the dewdrops from them scatters,
Breaking through the gossamer threads.
Dandelions' globous heads
Seem the gentle breeze to pray,
' Puff my feathered seeds away!'

Chafers to the leaves that cling
Strive to dry the draggled wing;
Admirals on bark of oak
Tarry till a sunny stroke
O'er their scarlet stripes and rings
Drinks the water from their wings.
Ladybirds with spots of black
On the rounded russet back,
Dash about, or linger sipping
Bells with fragrant honey dripping.

Now the redstart on a spray
Pipes, the shrike in jet and grey
Answers, and from throbbing throat
Bursts the throstle's bubbling note.

Forth strode Walter staff in hand,
Singing, straying through the land,
With a spirit light and gay
As each forest bird that day.
With the flower-heads he played,
As he through the meadows strayed;
Then he turned towards a hill,
Following a tinkling rill.

The Luck Flower.

Where the little pathway wended
Walter there the slope ascended,
Towards the mountain grey that towers
O'er that vale of meads and flowers;
Thinking, ' Now with sturdy strain
I the mountain-top may gain.'

With a cry of joy he stopped
Sudden, on his knee he dropped,
Peering underneath a braid
Of red roses, in whose shade,
Where through mosses ever weeping
Are the whispering waters creeping.
Thence the youth exulting drew
A flowret of the turquoise hue;
On his breast the plant he set,
With a feeling of regret
That, to glad another eye,
Friend or parent was not by.

Little then young Walter knew
The virtue of that blossom blue:
He the Flower of Luck had got—
The Wishing Wort, Forget me-not,

That blooms but for a single day
When summers seven have slipped away.
Not an iron bolt or lock,
Not an adamantine rock,
Can resist that flowret's shock ;
But before that herb of day
Stoutest bars and chains give way,
And the gaping rock reveals
Treasures which its womb conceals.
It can ope the prison cell,
Burst the barriers of Hell ;
Ay, to Heaven's gates applied,
Starts the crystal bar aside,
And the valves reel open wide !

Now himself the youth addrest,
With that blossom on his breast,
To the task of the ascent,
Forward on his ash-staff bent.
Higher up the mountain flank,
Through the vegetation rank,
Thus his pathway Walter broke
Through a coppice wood of oak ;
Where the wild-dove echoes woke.

The Luck Flower.

Then beneath a birchen shade,
Through a fragrant ferny glade,
Upward still a passage frayed,
On towards a rocky height
Where the saxifrages white
Patterned out a lace of light;
Up a rough and shattered edge
To a verdant cushioned ledge,
Where the sun was busy drying
Primulas that had been crying.
There he stood before a scar
Striking up, the way to bar
    To all further climbing.
From its rugged face it flung
Echoes of some bells that rung,
    In the valley chiming.
Thus the youth before it stood,
In distressed and doubting mood,
Seeking cranny, shelf or root,
Grasp for hand, support for foot,
Caught a tuft of purple stock,
Grappling, bosom to the rock.
Sudden, with a hollow moan,
As the Luck Flower touched the stone,

Formed a fissure, longer growing,
Shattered fragments downward throwing,
Waxing wider every minute,
And disclosing depths within it.
Then. O sight of awe and wonder!
With a gathering roar of thunder,
Yawned a cavern, access giving
To abysses no man living
E'er had seen.

          The youth amazed
Down the mighty passage gazed,
There beheld the gems, the gold
Mountains in their hearts enfold,
Garnered wealth, by man untold.
There the emeralds glimmered green,
Rubies glowed with crimson sheen,
Diamonds shot their coloured rays,
Red carbuncles were ablaze,
Amber topaz flickered bright,
Glowed the yellow chrysolite.
Varied gems, exhaustless store,
Crusted the vast caverns o'er;
Strewed with nuggets was the floor,

The Luck Flower.

Like to clots of dribbled gore
From the severed veins of ore,
Which were leaking still, and flowing
Streams of liquid gold were glowing.

In his hand his rod he clasped,
Down the passage Walter passed,
Full of trembling eagerness
Somewhat precious to possess ;
In a moment wealth to gain,
Without labour, care and pain.

In the mountain's womb he stands—
All is ready to his hands—
Round whichever way he turns,
Gold or precious crystal burns.
With a throbbing pulse he kneels,
And the glittering pebbles feels ;
Gathers drops of gold that fall
Trickling down the spangled wall ;
Chokes his pockets with gold dust,
Up his sleeves the gems are thrust,
Fills his cap with jewels rare,
Hitches diamonds in his hair.

In the bosom of his blouse
Puts some, others in his shoes.

Valued not, as down he stooped
From his breast the blue flower drooped,
And fell upon the glittering soil,
All unheeded midst the spoil.
Then, encumbered with his store,
Powerless quite to carry more,
Back towards the light of day
Walter slowly bent his way.
Hark! he heard a feeble sigh,
And a low imploring cry:
  'Forget me not! Forget me not!

Ah! what spake he little knew,
It was the magic flowret blue;
But he turned again and took
Round that mighty vault a look.
Misconstrued the voice that spoke,
From the side two gems he broke—
 Diamond drops like frozen tears—
And (filled each pocket, pouch and poke)
 Thrust the jewels in his ears.

The Luck Flower.

Once again the feeble sigh,
Once again the entreating cry,—
    'Forget me not! Forget me not!'
But, the voice no more discerned,
Towards the gate again he turned.

Then—a rumble, roar, a shock,
Bowed and reeled the living rock.
In his terror Walter fled,
Stones were falling round his head,
Right and left the gems he threw
As he towards the entrance flew,
Cast each diamond padded shoe,
Reached the gate, was nearly through—
Hark! a boom and burst of thunder,
  Reels the mountain with a crash,
  Then the sides together clash,
And the youth is cut asunder.

Friend! some little flower may lie
In hollows of thy memory,
That pleads to thee with earnest cry,—
    'Forget me not! Forget me not!'

Some little flower, not long to last,
Would mysteries ope long bolted fast,
If firmly to thy bosom claspt;
Some flower whose touch would open hurl
The heavenly gates of lucid pearl ;
Some little flower, that ne'er again,
Though sought in penitence and pain,
Once lost, thou ever canst regain—
    Forget it not ! Forget it not !

THE THREE CROWNS.

[LABATA, *Thesaurus Moralis.* Colon. 1652.]

'When the morning breaketh,
    Summon me for Prime;
When the white light waketh,
    Boy! the church-bell chime;'

Said the Priest, and wended,
    Weary, to his bed;
Laid upon his pillow
    Low his heavy head.

Sideways set Orion,
    Louting on one knee,
Holding up his cudgel,
    Dipping in the sea.

Slowly o'er the pine-tops
  Wheeled about the Bear;
All night long the water
  Whispered on the weir.

As the eyelid fluttered
  Of arousing dawn,
O'er the jagged horizon
  Threads of light were drawn,

Peering 'twixt the fir-boles
  Plastered with the snow,
Wan and white, uncoloured,
  Eastward, lying low.

Harshly from the tower
  Clamoured forth the bell,
Making morning slumbers
  Chequered where it fell.

Then the Friar, waking,
  Turned upon his side:
'Keenly cold is biting,'
  Muttered he, and sighed.

'There is scarce a glimmer
 Through the frosted pane;
Church is like a cellar;
 I will sleep again.'

Stood the little server,
 Waiting at the door,
Noting robin redbreasts
 Hopping in the straw.

'Had I but a riddle,
 Stick, and crumbs of bread,
I could catch these robins!'
 Eagerly he said.

But with sudden impulse
 Turned and sought the choir,
Touched the altar tapers
 With a flake of fire;

Opened wide a Psalter,
 And, in church alone,
Sang the Psalms of David
 To their ancient tone.

Once again Orion
    With a halting knee,
Brandishing his cudgel,
    Dived into the sea.

And above the fir-tops
    Wheeled again the Bear;
Whilst the water fretted
    Hoarsely o'er the weir.

Once again the jangle
    Of the bell for Prime
Told, at dusk of morning,
    Of awaking time.

By the mindful server
    Rung as he was bid,
Once again the Friar
    Raised his heavy lid:

' How the wind is wailing
    On the window pane!
Sweet are second slumbers,
    I must sleep again.'

But the little server,
   Looking forth, descried
Pools of water frozen,
   Offering a slide.

For a winter morning
   Better no device
Than, with tingling pulses,
   Whirling o'er the ice.

But, abruptly turning,
   Hied he to the choir,
Touched the altar tapers
   With a flake of fire;

Oped the great Church Psalter
   Standing up on toe,
Sang the Psalms of David
   Solemnly and slow.

Once again Orion
   Seaward with his flail
Set, and Ursus major
   Whisked about his tail.

But the tempest raging
    Hid the stars from sight,
And the falling snow-flakes
    Blotted out the light.

At the time for stirring
    Woke the little lad,
Cuddled in his blankets,
    Shuddering and sad.

'Must I on this morning
    Leave my bed so warm,
To struggle in the churchyard
    Through the snow and storm?

'Father John, I'll warrant,
    Lapped in slumber lies;
Twice has failed already:
    Wherefore should I rise?'

Yet from bed he started,
    And the Church bell rung,
Oped the Psalms of David,
    And the office sung.

All that while, in vision
    Lay the Priest, and saw,
Robed in light, the Saviour
    By the Heavenly Store,

Whence He had extracted
    That He now did hold
In His hand,—three jeweled,
    Burnished crowns of gold.

'These for me, my Master!'
    Cried the Priest with joy.
'No, my son!' He answered;
    'For the serving boy.

'Thrice has he been trièd,
    Thrice has he prevailed;
Crowns become the victor,
    Suit not him who failed.'

THE RABBI'S SON-IN-LAW.

[*Gittin*, 56. *Kethuboth*, 63. *Nedarim*, 49.]

I.

THE WEDDING OF AKIBA.

At the peeping of the morning
   Stood a damsel at the door
Of her father's barn, a plucking
   From her lover's locks the straw.

She was daughter of a Rabbi,
   Calba Shebua, far and wide
Known for wealth and lavish splendour,
   Noted for his boundless pride.

From her lattice often looking,
   She had watched her father's hind
On a wild-thyme slope reclining,
   As his nimble fingers twined

The Rabbi's Son-in-Law.

With the asphodel, the lily,
    Whilst the sheep about him lay
Dozing in the glowing splendour
    Of the cloudless summer day;

Or, beneath a fig-tree halting,
    Leaning on his shepherd's staff,
Where the pleasant water bubbled,
    That his thirsty flock might quaff.

When beside her window sitting,
    Through the rattle of her loom,
Flowed a lay of limpid gladness,
    Wafted lightly through the room,

Telling how the shepherd Jacob
    Tended Laban's herds so long
For the love he bore to Rachel.
    As she listened to the song,

Were her cheeks as damask roses,
    And her eyelids dripped with tears
At the thought of Jacob's waiting
    Through those weary fourteen years.

Once it fell at happy springtime,
   When the mowers mowed the grass,
And the tossing hay made fragrant
   Every zephyr that did pass—

That she went into the meadow;
   Akiba, the hind, was there
Blithely singing, with a sunbeam
   Tangled in his amber hair—

That she offered him a beaker
   Brimming o'er with Helbon wine;
In it lay the sun reflected
   With a ruby-crimson shine.

As the shepherd came towards her
   Were his cheeks with labour flushed,
Were his eyes as azure tarnlets
   Whence a stream of rapture gushed.
Mantling face and neck and bosom,
   Scarlet to her forehead rushed.

Trembled all the ruddy liquor
    When the flowing cup she set
In his fingers, stretched towards it;
    Then their hands and glances met.

Calba Shebua saw them standing,
    And he read the looks that burned
In their faces; and with fury
    Sudden on his daughter turned,
And he spat at her with loathing
    And with frenzy at her spurned.

Then he cast her from his household,
    And he cast her from her home,
And he bid her, with her shepherd,
    In her degradation roam.

And he sentenced her for ever
    From his presence to depart,
For he plucked her from his memory,
    And erased her from his heart.

Spoke the shepherd very calmly.
 'Then I call on the Most High
God of Abram, Isaac, Jacob!
 He will stand the orphan by;

'And before His sacred Presence
 Take I this sweet dove of thine,
Be thou witness, haughty Rabbi—
 And I make her wife of mine.

'For of thought or word unlawful
 Have I kept my conscience clear:
It is thou, in thy blind passion,
 Who bestow'st her on me here.

'Child of thine she is. Her portion
 I demand of thee. At least
Do thou deck the wedding chamber,
 And prepare the marriage feast.'

Cried the father, raging madly,
 'As her portion take my scorn;
For thy chamber, yonder outhouse;
 For thy feast, the husks of corn!'

II.

THE MORROW OF THE WEDDING.

As the morning star was waning,
  On the threshold of the door,
By the light, its power gaining,
    Ruth unravelled
  From the shepherd's locks the straw.

On the meadows rime was lying,
  In the valley, white and dead;
High a wakeful lark was flying;
    Dew was dripping
  From the thatching of the shed.

Peaks of Lebanon, outleaning,
  Caught the sun, and were aglow,
Like a rank of seraphs meaning,
    At a signal,
  To unfurl their plumes of snow.

So the damsel plucked, restraining
 With an effort from her eyes
Bitter showers of grief from raining,
 And repressing,
Resolutely, swelling sighs.

Akiba his bride so peerless
 Folded to his breast, and said,
' Hast thou courage? art thou fearless?'
 Softly stroking
With his hand her raven head.

' Thou hast one without a penny,
 One without a single friend,
One with kindred poor, if any:
 Unto such one,
Canst thou still thy love extend?

' When I see the tear-drops oozing,
 Do I count it as a sign
That the husband of thy choosing
 Cannot please thee,
But for home thou wilt repine?'

Then her arms so white and slender
    Weaved she quickly round his throat,
Lifting glances fervent, tender,
        On his lips
    She with hers the answer wrote.

Hung she thus with plaited finger,
    And the tears began to roll:
'Let me on thy bosom linger,
        Fondly breathing
    Into thee my burning soul.

'Husband, here I'd rest for ever,
    In a sweet untroubled calm;
Naught from thee thy Ruth should sever,
        Gathered closely
    In thy firm protecting arm.

'Every kiss should add fresh fuel
    To a blazing core of fire;
But such love to thee were cruel;
        I were selfish
    Yielding to my hot desire.

'Fare then forth, I bid thee, dearest,
    And acquire thyself a name:
She enjoins,—to thee thy nearest;
    Till, and sowing,
Thou shalt reap a crop of fame.

'From the arms of her thou prizest,
    Go to distant schools, and learn
What is taught,—the best, the wisest:
    That acquired,
Then to this true heart return.

'Husband! if I loved thee little,
    I would bid thee near me stay;
But self-seeking love is brittle,
    So I urge thee,
I adjure thee, fare away.'

Then her necklaces untwining,
    And the bracelets from her arm
Plucked she off, and diamonds shining
    From her fingers,
Laid she in the shepherd's palm.

'Think, my love, when thy hope flaggeth,
    When exhausted fails thy mind,
Think, when thy ambition laggeth,
       Of the dear one
    Who for thee remains behind.

'Think, when whitely morning shimmers,
    That her prayers for thee arise;
Think, when evening twilight glimmers,
       Turned to Zion,
    She for thee entreats the skies.

'Once again, heart's dearest, kiss me,
    Clasp me to thy loyal heart.
I shall need thee, thou wilt miss me;
       We are one
    Ever, though long leagues apart.'

The Rabbi's Son-in-Law.

III.

THE RETURN.

Fourteen suns their course have sped :
Spinning for her daily bread,
 Still an exile from her home,
Struggled Ruth with want to cope,
Waiting God's own time, in hope,
 But the shepherd did not come.

At her window, with her rock,
She is sitting ; tufts of stock,
 In a pitcher, scent the air.
As the sun upon her shines,
Mark the many silver lines
 Traced among the raven hair.

On this day a Rabbi great
Seeks the city in high state,
 With the pupils by him led.
There are gathered in the street
Citizens their guest to greet,
 Calba Shebua at their head.

Ruth but little heeds the throng,
Murmuring a plaintive song,
    As the spindle briskly twirls.
She is dreaming of a lad
With a shepherd's crook, who had
    Eyes of blue and amber curls.

But there bursts from her a sigh,
Starts the torrent to her eye,
    As her haughty father nears;
Falls the spindle, and the line
Of the flax that she doth twine
    Twinkles with her threaded tears.

With a glance of hard disdain,
Cutting her with cruel pain,
    At his daughter Calba stares.
O'er her work she bows her face,
Praying God would of His grace
    Soothe the anguish that she bears.

When she lifts her head, a shout
From the eager mob without
    Tells her he of high renown
Is approaching in the street.
Sounds the tramping of the feet
    As he passes through the town.

Slowly, midst a concourse great
Of disciples who did wait
    On the lessons that he taught,
Passed the Rabbi, tall and fair,
With blue eyes and amber hair,
    And a forehead full of thought.

Calba Shebua, his white head
Bending, with his hands outspread,
    Touching with his brow the ground,
Said, 'Oh! highest in repute,
Rabbi! we in thee salute
    Lofty wisdom, lore profound.

'Out of Jamnia * hath report
  Tidings of thy learning brought;
    Higher honour for our place
None than this, that thou shouldst deign
  Us to visit. Oh, remain,
    And our little city grace!

'We our servants, homes, and land,
  Rabbi! place at thy command,
    Only,—here with us abide!'
'Hold! disciples round me gather!
  Thou hast promised, ancient father,'
    Suddenly the stranger cried.

There was silence through the crowd:
Then he spoke, 'fore all, aloud,
  'Rabbi, hear me! wilt thou take
Me as inmate of thy house,
Give thy daughter as my spouse?
  Calba Shebua, answer make!'

---

* Jamnia, at the time of the Maccabees, was a large and populous haven. After the destruction of Jerusalem, it became the seat of the Rabbinical schools.

'Oh, how gladly!' faintly spoke
Calba, as suspicion broke
    Dimly on his troubled brain.
'Hear him!' Then the stranger turned
Whither long his heart had yearned,
    Thither now his fingers strain.

'My disciples! bend your glance
On my wife—in speechless trance,
    Leaning at yon open pane.
All I have, and all I know,
I to yonder woman owe,
    She gave all, that I might gain.

'Oh, true woman! holy, pure,
Ready meekly to endure,
    In thy sweet, unselfish love;
God-made woman! man were vile
But for thee to reconcile
    Him to labour; and to prove
Mainspring of all actions high,
Ready, impulse to supply,
    And his sluggish nature move.

The Rabbi's Son-in-Law.

'God-made woman! man may roam
Years from thee,—but thou art home,
 Whither with the olive leaf
Must his whitest longings wing,
And their purest treasures bring;
 Solace thou to every grief.

'Let me pass! in very truth,
Sighs my spirit after Ruth,
 Clear a passage to the door!
Back, sirs! we must meet alone,
That true heart is mine,—mine own.
 See! her dear eyes trickle o'er.

'Let me pass, to wipe those tears,
We have not met for fourteen years.
 If in all the mighty store
Of my learning garnerèd,
Aught is worthless——from my head
 Shall her fingers pluck the straw.'

THE MINER OF FALUN.

[AFTER TRINIUS.]

IN an ancient shaft of Falun
    Year by year a body lay,
God-preserved, as though a treasure,
    Kept unto the waking day.

Not the turmoil nor the passions
    Of the busy world o'erhead,
Sounds of war, or peace-rejoicings,
    Could disturb the placid dead.

Once a youthful miner, whistling
    Hew'd that chamber, now his tomb.
Crashed the rocky fragments on him,
    Closed him in abysmal gloom.

Sixty years pass'd by, ere miners
    Toiling, hundred fathoms deep,
Broke upon the shaft where rested
    That poor miner in his sleep.

As the gold-grains lie untarnish'd
    In the dingy soil and sand,
Till they gleam and flicker, stainless,
    In the digger's sifting hand;

As the gem in virgin brilliance
    Rests, till usher'd into day:
So, uninjured, uncorrupted,
    Fresh and fair the body lay.

And the miners bore it upward,
    Laid it in the yellow sun,
Up; from out the neighbouring houses
    Fast the curious peasants run.

Who is he? with eyes they question;
    Who is he? they ask aloud;
Hush! a wizen'd hag comes hobbling,
    Panting, through the wondering crowd.

Oh ! the cry—half joy, half sorrow—
    As she flings her at his side,
'John ! the sweetheart of my girlhood,
    Here am I, am I, thy bride.

'Time on thee has left no traces,
    Death from wear has shielded thee ;
I am aged, worn, and wasted,
    Oh ! what life has wrought on me !'

Then his smooth unfurrow'd forehead
    Kiss'd that ancient wither'd crone ;
And the death which had divided,
    Now united them in one.

HUMOROUS POEMS.

THE DREAM OF THE HALTER (7).

[*Mulierem alicui copulare, et crucem ei imponere prorsus idem est.*—
PACIUCHELLI *in Jonam*, lib. i. p. 272.]

'LAST night
I awoke in a fright,
After a horrible dream that I had,
A concatenation of all that is bad.
I thought
I was brought
Under a terrible gallows-tree:
The look was enough to stagger me.
The bells from the steeple
Were ringing, the people
In plenty were gathering round to see.
I shook in my shoes;
The cold clammy dews
Of the horror of death broke out on my brow:
I had not the pluck of a man, I allow.

The parson stood by
With a lacrymose eye,
But I'm sure was not half as disposed to cry
As was I.
And methought as I stood on the scaffold, the noose
Was fitted about me, at first rather loose,
But, tightening fast ;
Hope was leaving at last.
I struggled for freedom, but struggled in vain,
The fiercer the struggle, the tighter the strain
And the keener the pain.
O for a knife
To sever the cord!
To escape with my life!
For be well assured
I didn't let Hope fly away beyond hail,
Without a considerable tug at her tail.
Then,—sudden I uttered a deafening scream,
And——awoke from my dream.
Now you are a wizard. The Future you scan,
So you are the man
For the money I offer. Then prithee explain,
And rede me my vision, for wholly in vain
Have I battered my brain
To find the solution,—but all of my pain

Most fruitless has been.—
Well! what does it mean?
I am sure, I repeat, that the vision I had
Is a prognostication of something bad.'

Gravely, yet slyly, the wizard, he scann'd
The marks on the nails, the lines in the hand,
Then lifting his face he solemnly eyed
His inquisitive customer, ere he replied:
'I think it no wonder you're frightened and harried;
   The vision is clear;
   It means—do you hear?—
In the course of the week you are going to be married.'

THE TELESCOPE.

[' Qui tubi optici usum ignorant, si præpostere oculo adhibeant, objecta etiam e longinquo sita longissimo intervallo distare, arbitrabuntur. O peccator ! mortem quam longissime abesse credis? Adverte tuam imperitiam: tubum opticum secus adhibes, quam adhibere consueverant Sancti Dei. Disce ab his tubo uti.'—DE BARZIA, *Manductio ad Excit. Christianorum*, p. 52. August. Vend. 1732.]

JOHN BROWN and wife a-fairing went,
On business and on pleasure bent :
   He, to inspect some cattle,
She, to procure some household stuff—
A boa, crinoline, and muff—
   And taste some tittle-tattle.
John sold full well a drove of sheep,
And bought some bullocks middling cheap,
   After a wordy battle.
And Mistress Brown laid in some toys
For Bill and Joe, her precious boys,
   A pop-gun and a rattle.
Now when the fair was done, the weather
Held up, so John and wife together

The Telescope.

Walked through the fields to their abode,
Sending the cattle by the road.

Said John, 'How should you think, my lass,
That I have spent my extra brass,
  On self, not Joe or Billy?'
Then Mrs. B. with toss of head,
'This thing is certain, Brown,' she said,
  'It went on something silly.'
'Alack,' said Brown, 'upon my life
You are a thorough woman, wife,
  And rush at rash conclusions.
There is no silliness, I hope,
In purchasing a telescope,
  To see through vain delusions!
It makes the distant prospect clear,
Remotest objects bringeth near—
  My oath upon the Bible!'
Unluckily he had not learned
To use it, and he therefore turned
  The wrong end to his eyeball.
Sudden his wife cried, 'Oh, have done!
And, for your life, run, Johnny! run—
  Here comes a mad bull tearing.'

'Steady!' said John with lifted glass;
'Don't be uneasy, Betsy, lass!
   I'll take the mad bull's bearing.
Why! wherefore should you feel alarm?
A bull can never do one harm
   That still is ten miles distant.'

'O John, O John! I pray you fly!'
Brown, with the spyglass to his eye,
   Said, 'At the proper instant.'
'He's coming, lad! with lowered horn!'
Brown answered with a laugh of scorn,
   'He's five miles off at present.'

She fled at once, and refuge took
Beyond a paling, hedge and brook,
   Thus saved from aught unpleasant.
John, looking through his purchas'd toy
In confidence without alloy,
   Felt jocund as a linnet.
To Betsy's utterances of fear
He answered, 'When the bull is near,
   I'll fly that very minute.

The hedge and stream are close at hand,
And soon I shall in safety stand,
   I shan't take long in crossing.
He's now a mile off. Well! I'll run.'
—That instant, in the air he spun,
   Upon the bull's horns tossing.

I saw a damsel, giddy, gay,
Who fluttered through the sunny day
   Without a thought of sorrow,
With heightened colour, gilded hair,
In costly dress, and jewels rare,
   She looked not to the morrow.
'Old age creeps on,' I said, 'fond maid,
When all this pageantry must fade,
   What then?'—Without replying,
A colour to her forehead rushed
And mockingly she past me brushed
   With all her ribbons flying,
With jingling chains and rings. 'Alas!
You through the wrong end of the glass
   Are looking,' I said, sighing.

I saw a youth with reckless haste
Time, opportunities, and talents waste,

Whilst through a fortune racing.
' 'Ere ruin comes I will amend
And set myself to business, friend!'
   This madness is amazing.
The science of his glass unlearn'd
He also, with the spyglass turn'd,
   Is through the wrong end gazing.

I saw an aged usurer, deep
In reckonings plunged, whilst crouched to leap
   The King of Dread was nearing.
The old man little deemed that those
Accounts another hand would close,
   So laboured on unfearing.
Vainly attention to arrest I tried:
'O fool! one moment put aside
   The bargain you are booking.'
He would not lift his head. Alas!
He through the wrong end of the glass
   Incessantly was looking.

Dear little child! in opening youth
Acquire from me this solemn truth.

A truth all wisdom summing—
Learn how to use thy telescope;
Then, come what may, prepared, I hope,
  Thou wilt be for its coming.

DOCTOR BONOMI.

By chance
An alchymist doctor whose fortunes were down,
Shifted quarters, and set up one day in a town
    In France.
He hired a house, and affixed to the door
A name that the people had never before
    Seen.
The doctor was upright and stiff as a wall,
Remarkably bony, uncommonly tall,
    And lean.
Now into his house from a waggon was brought,
Whilst a crowd gathered staring, a monstrous retort;
And sweating and swearing, a staggering porter
Bore in a leviathan pestle and mortar;

Then hideous syringes, alchymical fixtures,
And great podgy bottles of all-coloured mixtures.
    A flutter
Among the gazers, who deemed every drop
Explosive material to go off with a pop
    And splutter.
Therefore the people kept back in the street
Ready to beat an immediate retreat,
Should the doctor a tendency show to be loading
The squirts, or the bottles give signs of exploding
    By fizzing.
Some gazed in mute awe on his spectacles big,
Whilst others the cut of his comical wig
    Were quizzing.
Unheeding, the doctor paced solemnly round
In silence that whispered of wisdom profound
    And vast.
But when all his chattels were carried within
    To the last,
The physician's grave features relaxed to a grin,
As he said, 'That will do; I think now I have nearly all
For this little city, the needful material.'
Now round with the speed of a fire, the report
Of the squirts, the great bottles, the tubes, the retort,

Flew;
And from every quarter the inquisitive pour,
Men, and of women, of course, a great store,
And the multitude fast round the alchymist's door
    Grew.
Sudden, the crier emerged with a horn,
Calling, 'O yes, O yes, this blessed morn
Into our city, of doctors e'er born
    The chief
Has come, Psalmanazar Bonōmi,
Physician extraordinary to the King of Dahomy.
A deeper read doctor no mortal can show me;
He's doctor of medicine of famous Louvain;
Salamanca boasts of him (Salamanca's in Spain);
And, to prove that his qualifications are thorough,
He passed at Montpelier, Bologne, Edinboro'.
    In brief
This alchymist-doctor of learn'd Salamanca
(Expressive though vulgar the term) is a spanker.
Now vain the delusion of him who supposes
The doctor sets plasters, lets blood, or gives doses,
Applies leeches, pounds powders, rolls pills, spreads a
    blister:
Far other, good people, the practice of Mister

Bonōmi.

Don't dream, if you're ill, for this doctor to send,
For certainly on you he will not attend.
Whatever your malady, be well assured,
You must not seek *him*, if you want to be cured.
Should he, like a common hack doctor, go round—
He the elixir of life who has found
    In Dahomy?
No! he visits not prince, noble, burgher, or peasant.
    Why should he? A score
    Of doctors and more
Are set up in this poky old city at present.
    So those who have croup,
    And those with the hoop,
And those who have cholera, liver complaint,
Rheumatics, lumbago, have bile, inflammation,
Influenza, or measles, have fits, or who faint,
Have fevers, convulsions, tic, gout, palpitation,
    Don't
Let them by calling Doctor Bonomi bother.
He will not attend; they must summon another;
Nor strive to induce, by a quadrupled fee,
Or by flattery, to bring him to visit, for he
    Won't.

But, when you have found all physicians to fail,
And every prescription has ceased to avail,
When the pulse beats no more, and the last sigh is sped,
When the last tear has trickled, the last word been said,
 When
Rigid the muscles, when motionless lies
The patient, sans breath, and sans ears, and sans eyes,
Sans feeling, sans thinking, sans all things, in bed ;
In a word, when you know that the patient is dead,—
 Then
Send for the illustrious Doctor Bonomi,
For then, in his own graphic words, " All will know me
 To be
The Only Physician who has any science,
The only Bonomi, with none in alliance,
Who sets all the doctors of France at defiance."
 So he
Urges all those of high rank or low station
By mortality robbed of a darling relation,
 Father or mother,
 Sister or brother,
Uncle or aunt, wife, husband, or lover,
And the same from the power of the grave would recover,

    Let 'em
Apply to the doctor at their earliest leisure,
And, if not engaged, it will give him great pleasure
For the trifling fee of five francs each—no more—
The precious departed to life to restore,
    And set 'em
In vigorous health once again in their places,
With their old dispositions, old habits, old faces.
So all who desire at a trumpery cost,
To recover a friend or relation that's lost,
Have only to come to the doctor, and he
Will their wishes attend at afore-mentioned fee.
    N.B.
A reduction to families, children half-price
Under twelve, and not according to size.'

Well, the doctor he waited, the crier he cried,
Newspaper notices, placards, were tried,
But the crying and waiting proved wholly in vain ;
And days as they passed, made it daily more plain
That folks were not eager to bring back again
    Those who had died ;
    For—*no one applied.*

So after the doctor a fortnight had waited,
    And nobody came,
He issued a poster, the colour of flame,
    Whereon it was stated
    That greatly to blame
Were the people for thinking that he was deceiving 'em;
And, therefore, before he determined on leaving 'em,
    He did intend
    At the week's end
To prove he had power to do what he said.
He would go to the churchyard and raise *all* the dead.
Now, scarce had the placard appeared in the street,
Ere there came to the door a loud clatter of feet,
    And one
Burst in on the doctor with colourless cheek,
And in his excitement scarce able to speak:
'Did you say you were going at the end of the week
To raise all the dead from the graves of the city?'
He fell on his knees wailing, 'Doctor, have pity!
    Do not arouse
    My slumbering spouse!
    Though fun
To a stranger such practices may be,
They're death and perdition, and worse, sir, to me.

If my wife,
Who is dead—rest her soul!—came to life,
What should I do?
For scarce had I seen her in sepulchre laid
Ere I put in the banns, and was spliced to her maid.
It never would do
Wives to have two,
Especially when the first wife was a scold,
Corpulent, fussy, and ugly and old;
And after her death one's enjoying her gold
With Kitty,
Who is dapper, and young, and good-natured, and pretty.'
Then he pressed
A well-weighted purse on Bonomi, and said,
'Now, doctor, remember, in raising the dead,
Let *her* rest.'

Now scarce had this gentleman taken his hat,
When there pealed on the door a loud rat-a-tat-tat.
Then in came another man, shaking and bowing,
With forehead perspiring, and cheeks all a-glowing,
Who said, in an accent of trouble and fear,
Whilst with a blue handkerchief mopping his face,
'Why, doctor! good heaven! is it true what I hear,

That you're going to raise all the dead in the place?
Why, bless me! my uncle has lately deceased
    And left me his heir,
    And, dear sir, I declare
That now, from pecuniary troubles released,
I'm only beginning life's pleasures to taste.
Oh, doctor! if you've not the heart of a stone,
Have pity, and leave my poor uncle alone.
I pray you accept of this trifle, and save
Me the terrible blow.   Let *him* rest in his grave.'

Then in came another, with face of despair,
Who said palpitating, ' I pray you forbear!
My brothers are dead, I'm enjoying their share
Of the fortune my father amassed; I don't care
To have to refund it, surrendering the pelf;
It's a thousand times better to spend it oneself.
    Beside
Providence knew, I am sure, what was best,
When, by measles, it took my dear brothers to rest.
    They died
By Heaven's decree; and shall mortal perverse
Adventure what Providence rules to reverse?

  They are better by far,
  I'm convinced, where they are
(Here, doctor, I pray you to finger this purse);
  Earth was no home
For souls such as theirs, so the heavenly flame
Rose to the ether sublime whence it came.
O monster inhuman! rerivet again
Of spirit and matter the long-shatter'd chain!
Replace the poor bird in the cage whence it's flown!
Cast once more from his home the poor exile restored!
O'er the criminal pardoned again lift the sword!
For my brothers' sake, doctor, give ear to my plain,
  And let *them* alone.'

The next to appear was a lady, who said,
With pattering tears, and pendulous head,
  'Alack
For my master who lay for a long time in bed!
A terrible sufferer, whilst by his side
I tenderly waited and watched, till he died;
And must he, with every fond fancy and whim,
  Come back?
For years I kept dancing attendance on him,

And only when I was released by his death,
The leisure obtained to look round, and take breath.
    Now I enjoy,
    Without any alloy,
My freedom and income, which he, ere he died,
In return for my nursing took care to provide.
O, doctor! I'm tired of being a nurse:
So I pray you to take a few coins from this purse,
    And save
My feelings, by letting *him* rest in his grave.'

The next to arrive was a gentleman eager,
With sharp-pointed nose, long, lanky, and meagre;
    Like a rat's
Was his face. He, the tallest of hats
With the smallest of brims in his fingers was holding,
Whilst the stiffest cravat his long neck was enfolding;
His swallow-tails hung to the calf of his leg.
Now thus, in shrill tones, began he to beg,
    Making a bow:
'How do you do, doctor? how
Are you? dear doctor Bonomi; I'm calling
   To assure you I fear the event of a riot
In the city at the prospect, no little appalling,
    Of our dead folk not being allowed to lie quiet.

Dr. Bonomi.

I have come to you, doctor, in hopes to impress
Your mind with a sense of the prevailing distress
Which is caused among many good folk by the thought
Of the miracle which is about to be wrought.
But perhaps you will best understand, if I place
Before you an instance, a representative case.
  My lady gave birth
  Twice to twins ; in the earth
They are lying, very much to their benefit surely,
And to my satisfaction. They always were poorly;
  And, because of their ailing,
  They never ceased wailing,
  Till their happy release
  Gave the family peace.
They are well where they are; but, I fear and suppose,
With the others these babies to revive you propose.
What moneys they'll cost me in victuals and clothes!
Why, to think, sir,' he added, with agonised groan,
' Of the cost of four little boys' breeches alone,
Which always give way at the seat and the knee;
  Which they are ever outgrowing ;
  Which take buttons and sewing !
Alas! but four boys would be ruin to me.
They would always be yelping for something to eat ;
They wou'd cost me a fortune in bread, sir, and meat.

Then their education
　　　Befitting their station !
I have children already, enough and to spare.
Already my wife has found grey in my hair.
At the prospect I'm ready to die of despair
　　　Of having to provide
For four hungry, howling, nude creatures beside.
Therefore, good sir, if you wake those that sleep,
Clear of my babies I pray you to keep.
Here's a humble reminder, fifteen louis-d'or :
And, in raising the dead, pray, *my babies* pass o'er.'

Now was heard in the street of wheels a loud rumble ;
Then a sudden portentous loud rap at the door.
　　　And next, up the stair,
　　　With tumble
　　　And grumble
Full into the room came bouncing the Mayor.
'Ahem !' said his worship.　'Sacré bleu ! mille diables !
Are you going to arouse from their graves all the rabble ?
Are you, sir, the man who will quicken the dead ?'
He stopped, out of breath, but still waggled his head,
　　　Puffing and blowing.
'What !　Such an infringement of order, indeed!

Revolution and anarchy certain to breed.
 Do you think I am going
To tolerate it for one moment ? Odds bobbin !
To pay Peter, in verity, Paul 't would be robbing ;
For I fear I should have to vacate my great chair,
If, among all the others, you roused the ex-Mayor.
So, out of the city I bid you be packing,
Or me, ventre gris ! sir, you will not find lacking
In putting in force the full weight of the law,
And sending you where you were never before—
Into prison ; and mark you, if once you were in it,
You would not be able to slip out in a minute.
But I'm generous, doctor, and ready to offer
A compromise. Here are rouleaux in this coffer :
Take them. Your absence—I'm ready to buy it ;
Only, for mercy's sake, leave the dead quiet.
To the money you're welcome—accept, and be gone ;
But, whatever you do, leave the *ex-Mayor* alone.
 Now pack
Up your traps ; it's a beautiful morning
For shifting your quarters. No slighting my warning !
Why,' added his worship, with iciest stare,
' I'm 'whelmed with amazement to think you should dare
To dream of unseating ME—me, sir, the Mayor !

  Then back
With your bottles and drugs to the wilds of Dahomy,
There practise at ease, on fresh corpse or old mummy,
  With nothing to fear,
  But only not here.
So! out of the town with you, Doctor Bonomi!'

LIGHTENING THE VESSEL. (8)

[JOHANNIS RAULINI *Itinerarium Paradisi*, A.D. 1482: *De Matrimonio*, Sermon vii.]

A TERRIBLE storm on the ocean lay,
    And the waves ran mountains high;
The lightning flashed, and the thunder crashed,
    As Erebus was the sky.

A vessel was running before the blast
    With a rent and flapping sail,
She was hardly pressed and sore distressed
    With the fury of the gale.

The Captain was standing upon the deck,
    And wond'ring if hope were vain
After that night to behold the light
    Awake in the east again.

On board the vessel were bales of silk,
    And barrels of shining gold,
And pigs of lead were lying in bed
    At the bottom of the hold.

But there was a risk of other sort
    Than cargo, vessel, or life,
For the Captain had brought away from port
    Madam Malone—his wife.

Mistress Malone in the cabin sat,
    Sipping a cup of tea;
Whilst Captain Malone was wet to the bone
    In battling with the sea.

Mistress Malone had a nimble tongue,
    That sharper and freer grew;
And never a day but she nagged away,
    For she was an awful shrew.

The boatswain, approaching the Captain, said,
    Touching his cap: 'We are lost,
Unless you agree that into the sea
    The cargo shall be toss'd.

'I can lose my money and lose my time,
　　But life I cannot afford,
　So out let us fling the heaviest thing
　　That we can find on board.'

　The Captain he stood and bit his thumb
　　With a frowning brow a while;
　At last he said, with a jerk of the head,
　　And the symptoms of a smile :—

'Heavy indeed are the bales of silk,
　　And heavier is the gold,
　But heavier yet is the lead, I bet,
　　Lumbering in the hold.

'But there is a weight outweighs them all,
　　The heaviest I can find,
　More ponderous than lead, it crushes my head
　　And oppresses my soul and mind;

'Upon my spirit it ever lies,
　　In company, or alone.
　Come, boatswain, with me, and into the sea
　　We'll topple old Madam Malone!'

EX NIHILO NIHIL FIT. (9)

[*Itinerarium Paradisi: De Matrim.* Serm. vii.]

A YOUNG man sought his parish priest
The day before the village feast,
   To gather his advice.
'I'm sick of being celibate,
To-morrow I shall seek a mate
   And you the pair shall splice.
But, Parson ! I shall meet a batch
Of lasses. Which am I to catch,
   So many being nice ?

'There's Mary Jane has roses red,
And Bessie has a shrewdish head,
   And Susan has some money.

Ex Nihilo Nihil fit.

And Josephine is such a cook,
And Isabel is great at book,
    But Polly is so funny.
And Laura has such dancing eyes,
Phœbe's are calm as summer skies,
    And Siss is always sunny.

'And Grace has temper ever sweet,
And Anne is frank whene'er we meet,
    And modest Rose is shy,
And Nelly, she's the girl to dance,
And Rhoda casts a longing glance
    At me as I go by.

'But, Parson! how am I to find,
Among so many to my mind,
    The one to be my wife?
I cannot marry all, full well
I know; but *which* I cannot tell,
    I can't, Sir! on my life!

'The roses red of Mary Jane
  May languish with old age or pain,
    And Bessy's shrewdish head
  Might make *her* master, so I think,
  And so might Susan's chink-a-chink,
    The honeymoon once fled.

'And Josephine the cook might turn
  Her hand to grill, and baste, and burn
    Her husband. Isabel
  Might leave her book to lecture me,
  And Polly's fun directed be
    At chaffing me, as well;

'And Laura's dancing eyes might light,
  So giddy, on some other wight;
    Whilst Phœbe's tranquil eyes
  Some bad propensity may hide,
  For waters deep do stillest glide;
    And Siss, like summer skies,

'May cloud and flash with angry light,
When company is out of sight,
 And Grace's temper sweet
At home may fast acidulate;
And Anne, forgetful of her mate,
 Might frankly others greet.

'And modest Rose may have a thorn
That lurks beneath her shyness, worn
 To hide it; as for Nell,
Perhaps, instead of work, she'd dance;
And as for Rhoda's longing glance,
 It may be all a sell.

'But, Parson, you my nature know;
I'm amiable, but rather slow,
 Of wisdom have no grain.
At school the master always said
That I had got an empty head
 Of reason and of brain.

'In innocence I'm quite a child;
  In temper I am bland and mild,
    And butter won't dissolve,
Poor fool I am! upon my tongue.
Now therefore pray, for me, who'm young,
    My difficulty solve.
If I should wed a girl with sense,
She'd soon discover I was dense,
    And speedily revolve

'About her finger, me—as twine,
And I'd be her's, not she be mine,—
    She mistress, I her man.
Her love for me would quickly cool,
She'd treat me only as her fool,
    Or puppet stuffed with bran.

'I think I'd better pick, don't you?
  A lady minus just a screw,
    And softer than myself.
I'd rather like a pretty face,
And laughing eyes, and ease, and grace,
    And I could pocket pelf;

'But first and foremost, I must find
A woman without trace of mind,
    If I would rule my house.
Indeed, I cannot any way,
Content, the second fiddle play
    To satisfy a spouse.'

The Parson mused, and looking grave,
Rebukingly the answer gave :
    'No, no ! in verity !
For, if a baby came, my lad !
It would not do, 'twould be too bad
    Upon posterity.

'A foolish pair would surely breed
Most foolish offspring to succeed :
    What else could you expect ?
'But, Father ! Nature doth abhor
A vacuum, and it would store
    My child with intellect,

'And our deficiencies supply
And make our child a prodigy,
If only we had one.'
'The girl who's sensible and wise
She only is your proper prize,
Take her, or marry none.'
Deliberately the Parson spake :
'Two negatives will never make
A positive, my son !'

THE SENTENCE ON THE THIEF. (10)

[*Itinerarium Paradisi: De Matrim.* Serm. xi.]

A NOTABLE thief of Rotterdam,
    The worry of all the city,
Was taken at last, and made doubly fast
    In the prison, with scanty pity.

Excitement arose to boiling point,
    And folk would take no denial,
But were all agreed, to have indeed,
    In the market-place the trial.

The magistrates said, ' It may terror strike
    In the guilty, and embolden
The innocent ; so be content,
    It shall be publicly holden.'

The day arrived, and the mighty crowd
    Their way to the market fought,
For the people all, both great and small,
    Rejoiced that the thief was caught.

The judge was seated in scarlet cloak,
    The officers quelled disorder;
Lawyers were there, with preoccupied air,
    And the clerk, and the recorder.

Witnesses came, were questioned and heard,
    And the culprit felt with fear,
And a pallid face, that his ugly case
    Was made uncommonly clear.

And when the moment of sentence came,
    The judge to the people turned:
'Some have had life by this felon's knife
    Taken, and some have had burned

'Their houses, and all have something lost,
    Or suffered from him some way;
So I direct that you shall elect
    The penalty he shall pay.'

The Sentence on the Thief.

'Death!' they cried, 'is what we decide,'
    Yelling in ecstasy;
But how carried out, the turbulent rout
    In no way could agree.

Said one man, 'Let him suspended be
    As a warning from the steeple;'
But another said, 'Let us cut off his head,
    In the presence of the people.'

Said another, 'There is a sweeter sport,
    The breaking upon the wheel.'
Said another man, 'There's a better plan,
    The chopping to bits with steel.'

Said another: 'I've heard in good old times
    That culprits were stewed in oil.'
Said one, 'He shall bake;' and one, 'At the stake
    He shall roast;' said another, 'Boil.'

Then slowly arose from his seat the judge,
    And said, 'If you can't agree,
Then lend me your ear, and you shall hear
    A suggestion made by me.

'What sort of pain would you give the man—
    Continuous, or soon past?'
Then shouted all, both great and small,
    'Long, long, sir, may it last!'

'Would you rack his body and heart and mind,
    Or only rack him in part?'
They shouted all, both great and small:
    'Body and mind and heart!'

'Would you make him pray for a quick release,
    Or close his life with a blow?
Should he greatly desire Purgat'ry fire,
    As relief from present woe?'

They shouted all, both great and small:
    'Protract a tormented life!'
Said the Judge, 'Very well: to the criminal
    I here make over my wife.

'I could wish my enemy nothing worse
    Than a course of matrimonie
With that creature so grim in visage and limb
    Who has fastened herself on me.

'Shall this be the sentence I proclaim?'
　　The criminal gave a groan.
'Shall the woman be, who worries me,
　　The culprit's worry alone?'

The people all, both great and small,
　　Shouted: 'We so decide!'
Said the Judge, 'For thee I feel pity:
　　Criminal! claim thy bride.

'Happier far had death been thine,
　　And now to have yielded breath,
Than saddled to be with a ghoulish She
　　Through a lingering, living death.'

NOTES.

Note (1), page 26.

In 'Talmud Berachot' the Rabbi is called Akiba. In 'Taanith,' Tract III. 21, his name is Nahum.

Note (2), page 33.

'Talmud Jerusalem,' Haggada II. Halacha 1; 'Talmud Babylon,' Haggada II. fol. 15; 'Midrash Rabba,' Ruth iii. 13, and other places. I have taken great liberties with this tale. In its original form it is as follows. Meir and the apostate entered the school. Then said Elisha to the nearest lad: 'Repeat your lesson.' The boy replied, in the words of Isaiah lvii. 21. Elisha asked the second, and he repeated Ps. l. 16; then he rushed from the school. But Meir went after him with the words, 'Thou leadest men to destruction; again thou sayest, Turn again, ye children of men.' (Ps. xc. 3.) Then Elisha burst into tears, and died. After his burial, an uneasy flame danced on his grave; but Rabbi Meir laid it by repeating over the tomb the words of Ruth iii. 13.

Note (3), page 40.

The Archbishop is said to have been Jacques de Voragine, author of the famous 'Legenda Aurea,' but with injustice. See the introduction to 'La Légende Dorée,' Paris, 1843.

Note (4), page 50.

Cæsarius Heisterbachensis, lib. ii. c. 10. I have, however, somewhat altered the story of gossiping Cæsarius. His tale is this: 'Parisiis erat juvenis quidem in studio, qui suggerente humani generis inimico, talia quædam peccata commiserat, quæ obstante erubescentia nulli hominum confiteri potuit. Tandem, miserante Deo, in adolescente timor verecundiam vicit. Veniens ad Sanctum Victorem, priorem vocavit, et quia confitendi gratia venisset indicavit. Ille paratus ad tale officium, statim venit, in loco ad hoc deputato sedit, præmissaque exhortatione juvenem confiteri volentem expectavit. Tandem hora eadem pius Dominus cordi ejus contulit contritionem, ut quotiens confessionem inciperet, toties singultibus intercepto vox deficeret, in oculis lacrimæ, suspiria in pectore, singultus erant in gutture. Hæc vidit Prior, dicebat scholari: Vade scribe peccata tua in schedula, et defer ad me. Placuit consilium juveni, abiit scripsit, die altera rediit, et si confiteri posset iterum tentans, ut prius defecit. Et cum nil proficeret, schedalam Priori porrexit. Legit Prior et obstupuit, dixitque juveni: Non sufficio tibi solus dare consilium. Vis ut ostendam Abbati? et licentiavit ei. Venit Prior ad Abbatem, et porrexit schedulam legendam, rem ei per ordinem exponens. Quid denique gestum sit, audiant peccatores et consolentur. Mox enim ut Abbas chartulam ad legendum aperuit, totam ejus continentiam deletam invenit. Impletumque est in eo, quod Dominus per Isaiam dicit: Delevi ut nubem iniquitatem tuam, et ut nebulam peccata tua.'

Note (5), page 58.

Paciuchelli, 'Lect. Morales in Jonam.' This is a curious book: three folio volumes of commentary on the four chapters of Jonah. It is a storehouse of anecdote, legend, and fable. The tale I have versified runs thus in the original (tom. ii. p. 196): 'Legimus in vita Sancti Vedasti cæcum quendam, ubi sacra ossa in digniorem locum transferebantur, rogasse, ut reddito luminum usu sanctas episcopi reliquias intueri posset; vix preces effuderat, et quantocyus restitutos sibi oculos esse expertus est. Obstupuit, et secum hunc discursum efformavit : sed quis scit, an luminum usus ad animæ meæ salutem expediat? Inconsiderata nimis fuit mea petitio, cum debitas conditiones non adhibuerim. Quid egit? ad preces rediit : Domine! per Sancti tui Vedasti merita supplex rogo, ut si ea res animæ meæ saluti minus conducat, redeat infirmitas. Et ecce, eodem sane momento novâ caligine obducti sunt precantis oculi.'

Note (6), page 69.

Cæsarius Heisterbachensis, lib. x. c. 58. The story is told by this author of storks : 'Apud Cistercium, ubi caput est ordinis nostri, plurimæ nidificant cyconiæ. Quod ideo a fratribus religiosis permittitur, quia per illas non solum monasterium, sed omnia circuitu loca ab immundis vermibus mundantur. Hyeme appropinquante recedunt, et tempore certo redeunt. Die quadam cum acies suas ordinassent ad peregrinandum, ne hospitalitatis concessæ immemores esse viderentur, conventum qui eadem hora in agro laborabat petentes, eumque crebrius grutillando circumvolantes, omnes in admirationem verterunt, ignorantibus quid peterent. Ad quos Prior : Puto quod licentiam petant recedendi. Elevansque manum benedixit eis. Mox mirum in modum cum multa alacritate simul avolantes, monachis exeuntibus in viam qui regularem benedictionem accipere sive expectare parvipendunt, magnam verecundiam incusserunt.'

Note (7), page 153.

'Somniabat quispiam se cruci affigi: quare cùm petiisset quid tam triste, et infaustum prognosticon indicaret? Respondit Artemidorus Baldianus (lib. ii. c. 28): Viro uxorem non habenti, nuptias prædicere. Ergone somnium crucifixionis futurarum nuptiarum indicium est? Omnino: quia tantæ sunt miseriæ, labores, calamitates, et molestiæ quæ hunc statum comitantur, ut idem videatur uxorem ducere, et cruci affigi.'

Ribadeneira also relates (Histor. Prium Generalium, lib. iii. c. 17) that Didacus Lainez, second general of the Jesuit order, being filled with the most earnest desire of self-immolation, sought out how he could best 'take up his cross daily,' and conceived the surest manner would be in taking to himself a wife; for, says Ribadeneira, 'it seemed to him impossible in this world to find any cross heavier to lay upon himself, than a wife: consequently he hesitated whether he would not best fulfil the divine mandate by seeking a wife, it being impossible for him to embrace a more intolerable cross.'

Note (8), page 177.

Johannis Raulini, 'Itinerarium Paradisi,' Antw. 1612, p. 283: 'Cum quidam esset in navi onerata cum uxore sua litigiosa, et propter tempestatem necesse esset alleviare navem, et projicere merces in mari; cum projicerentur, rogavit ille ut etiam uxor sua projiceretur, asserens nihil esse tam onerosum sibi sicut uxor sua, et quod si eam haberent portare super humeros suos sicut, ipse, quod esset prior quæ in mari projiceretur.'

Note (9), page 180.

Itin. Parad. p. 286: 'Quidam galandus ad suum curatum accessit, dicens quod volebat nubere, et quod curatus sibi provideret de una uxore, dummodo tres haberet conditiones, scilicet, quod esset dives, quod pulchra, et quod non haberet caput, eo quod ipse malum caput haberet. Cui Curatus: Immo oportet quod habeat caput, quia vos habetis malum caput, et ipsa similiter habebit: et ex duobus capitibus duris et malis liquefactis in fornace, fiet unum bonum caput.'

Note (10), page 187.

Itin. Parad. p. 309. 'Accidit in civitate illa ut caperetur maleficus et latro pessimus, qui multos de civitate spoliaverat, et occiderat. Cumque cives quererentur, et judex a singulis consilium quæreret qualiter latro ille magis torqueri valeret, quibusdam dicentibus: Distrahatur caudis equorum, et suspendatur; aliis dicentibus: Igne cremetur: cæteris consulentibus ut vivus excoriaretur: cum perventum est ad alium qui malam habebat uxorem, respondit: Date illi uxorem meam; non video qualiter ipsum magis affligere valeatis.'

www.ingramcontent.com/pod-product-compliance
Lightning Source LLC
Chambersburg PA
CBHW020859230426
43666CB00008B/1243